My Arctic Summer

My Arctic Summer

AGNIESZKA LATOCHA

Translated by

Monika Cesarz

Whittles Publishing

Published by
Whittles Publishing Ltd.,
Dunbeath,
Caithness, KW6 6EG,
Scotland, UK

www.whittlespublishing.com

ISBN 978-184995-044-2

Printed by
Ashford Colour Press Ltd

CONTENTS

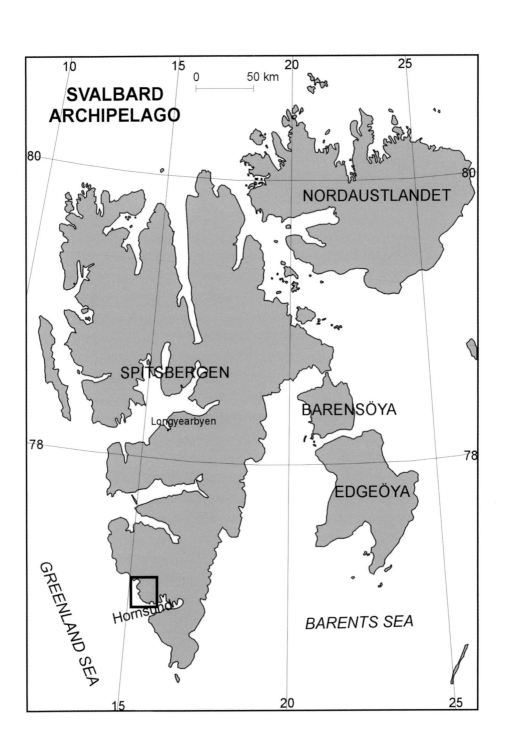

INTRODUCTION

Pebbles and mountains, at some spots marshes, arctic moss, rain and tåke,
the everlasting wind, in the winter constant drifting of the ice.
I am stuck in all this, cold and freezing and don't know why.
In the winter we are close to death.
However, at the same time aren't we close to life?
Maybe this is it, if you ask for an explanation.

There are places on Earth which you cannot abandon easily,
landscapes which impress you so much, that you are compelled to come back.

Per Olof Sundman, *The Arctic Ocean*

Spitsbergen, located about 1,200 kilometres from the North Pole, is the largest island of the Svalbard archipelago, which is situated between the Greenland Sea and Barents Sea. In administrative terms Svalbard constitutes an autonomous territory of Norway.

The first people to ever reach its shores were most probably the Vikings in the 12th century, who called it Svalbard—meaning 'cold shore'. In the 16th century the islands were 're-discovered', this time by Barents' expedition, who called them Spitsbergen—'pointy peaks'. In the centuries to come the archipelago was used primarily as a base for hunting whales as well as polar bears, foxes, seals and walruses. In the early 20th century coal deposits were found in some areas. This discovery began the mining history of the region. Beginning from the second half of the 18th century, the first scientific and research expeditions started to come to the shores of Svalbard. The

Poles joined the circle of Arctic explorers in the first half of the 20th century. It came as a result of the signing of the Svalbard Treaty by Poland in 1920, which enabled all signatory states to freely explore the archipelago islands and conduct scientific research. Numerous polar expeditions organised by the Poles encompassed worldwide projects, such as International Polar Year 1932–33, International Geophysical Year 1957–58 and International Polar Year (March 2007–March 2009). All this resulted in creating a very strong tradition of Polish research in the Arctic. At present, the research is carried out all year long at the Stanislaw Siedlecki Polar Station of Polish Academy of Sciences, in Hornsund, Spitsbergen, and seasonally in four field research stations run by different Polish universities. The explorers deal with a very extensive range of issues including flora and fauna, geological features, natural phenomena, environmental protection, etc. Spitsbergen is a magnet attracting specialists in various areas, from microbiologists to astrophysicists.

Heavy transport at the Polish Polar Station in Hornsund.

One might ask what is all this research about. Why carry out such extensive exploration so far away from home? Apart from sheer curiosity and the desire to understand the world and its natural laws, there are other answers to this question: answers that can be found in the past and answers that are yet to come. We talk about the past because thousands of years ago the territory of Poland was covered by massive layers of ice, the same as today's Arctic; the climate was much the same and similar processes were at work. These remote times can still be traced in today's landscape of my country. However, to thoroughly understand these processes we must head for the distant North, and see how they come into being and how they operate. The answers yet to come concern global climate changes – an issue that has become so topical and fashionable in recent years. Polar areas are particularly susceptible to all kinds of environmental changes. By examining certain phenomena, such as the pace of alteration in the size of glaciers, we can predict potential consequences of future changes and analyse the impact they will have on other parts of the world.

The results of research and scientific analysis have already been presented in many serious magazines and publications. But this is not what this book is about. My intention was first of all to convey the atmosphere of this special place in the North, so far away, but at the same time so close to Polish hearts. The book is hence an impression, showing, on the one hand, the world of Arctic nature, and on the other hand, the world of complex human relations that are forged in a small group in demanding conditions. This book does not contain a chronological description of one particular expedition, but it compiles events and pictures from three different journeys (from the summers of 2004, 2005 and 2007). Each chapter has its own individual keynote. The text includes no surnames, titles, scientific degrees, staff hierarchy, etc., as they are not as important as the spirit of the community.

Some of you may think the book idealises the polar world and I would agree. It was intentional. Why? you might ask. Firstly, because the human mind has this fortunate ability to remember everything that is good and retain positive images. Secondly, because good things need to be shown and emphasised since the contemporary world is doing everything to bombard us with bad news and negative emotions. There is good in each of us but very often it goes unnoticed. Extreme conditions, like these in Spitsbergen, trigger all kinds of emotions and reactions – good and bad. I write about both, but purposefully try not to expose the latter. It is enough to mention that they occur – just as in everyday life. However, I will deliberately stress everything that is good and beautiful in people, and what we humans are capable of doing in hardship or danger when only cooperation with others can save us.

The book records my personal memories but I do hope that the reflections therein will have a universal character. We all share the same needs, emotions, desires and reactions irrespective of the latitude we inhabit. Hopefully, for those who visit the Arctic regularly this book will be a reminder of their own experiences and adventures, while for anyone who has not yet been there, it will open a window on the world of Arctic nature and let them feel joy and the adventure of polar exploration.

❀ ❀ ❀

It all depends on people. Our travel memories are shaped by people, both co-participants of the expedition and acquaintances we meet by chance. I was lucky to come across a lot of kind and friendly people on my Arctic trips. I want to thank them all for my positive memories as they all contributed greatly to them.

My special thanks go to Krzysiek Migala, an experienced explorer of the polar regions, for his commitment as well as critical and factual comments that have definitely improved the initial version of the book.

I would like to also thank my parents for their infinite patience with their daughter's literary inclinations and aspirations, and especially my Mum – the first literary reviewer of freshly born texts.

Agnieszka Latocha

1 Beginning

We are certain that at the seas and lands of the far North, in the broad big world,
new expeditions will come up to work for the science
and for the good of mankind under the banner of Poland.

Stanislaw Siedlecki, *Amidst Polar Deserts of Svalbard*

The island below was veiled in thick clouds. Not a glimpse of a peak, glacier or coastline. What a shame that the Arctic is giving us such a cold welcome. Such an inhospitable land! The plane started to duck into the layer of grey clouds. It was just before landing that the world emerged again from obscurity and nothingness. It was exactly how I felt about it, as did my companions. It was our first expedition to the far North. The Arctic had not seemed real to us before. It was just an idea, an image, a destination. It was the main character in the stories told to us by senior colleagues who had contributed, for many years, to Polish research history in Spitsbergen. The stories sounded like fairy tales about some exotic land that might exist somewhere, but was completely beyond our reach – that is what we thought several years ago – and thus it was practically non-existent. Now, under the wheels of the landing plane, that vague idea became reality. And reality hit hard. We could feel it when the plane stopped abruptly with a jerk. We were welcomed by the wind that was sweeping the whole apron area of the small airport in Longyearbyen, the biggest town in the Svalbard archipelago.

In each part of the world the air has a different scent. You are struck by it with great force on your arrival and then you stop noticing it because you are submerged in it.

However, that first moment is like a scented visiting card of a country or continent. You will be greeted by a different smell or fragrance at the airports of India, Africa or Europe. The Arctic air smelled of coolness, freshness and the sea. You can never forget this first impression; you cannot mistake such scent for any other. The scent of open, vast areas, full of ice and rocks, which you are going to miss so much on your return to the concrete jungle of urban civilisation at lower latitudes.

So here we go: our elusive dreams have come true. It's become possible.

'Get on, get on! Drop your backpacks into the boot!' Jarek (pronounced 'Yarek'), nicknamed 'Rabbit', is a representative of a small Polish community in Spitsbergen. He has helped his fellow countrymen who come to Spitsbergen with logistics services for many years. He picks us up at the airport and drives us to the waterside of the harbour, where we are going to board the ship *Horizon II*.

The bus fills up with several groups of Polish people, polar enthusiasts or fanatics, who come from various scientific centres in Poland and are not sorry to change summer sunshine at home for the cold and drizzle of Spitsbergen. They are going to spend the summer and autumn months doing intense research on the Arctic environment. The ship will give us a lift to some hideaway places, researchers' lairs and after several weeks or months it will come back to collect us from different destinations where we were willingly stranded.

Most of the seats on the bus are taken as we set off towards the harbour.

'You surely know that the situation with the ice pack is still serious? The whole access to Hornsund[1] from the sea is blocked by the ice. All attempts made by boats to come into the fjord have failed so far. I don't want to ruin your good mood but you must take this into consideration. It may fail this time, too.'

Such was the welcoming speech made by Uve, the boss of the Polar Station of Polish Academy of Sciences. It certainly wasn't optimistic. 'We now reckon that *Horizon II* has only a one per cent chance of arriving in Hornsund port.'

One per cent. It definitely sounded grave. But we must stick to this one per cent and believe that everything will turn out all right. We can't doubt it. One per cent still provides hope. We must succeed.

Of course, we have heard about the blockade. We knew about it back home. The southern edges of Spitsbergen were blocked by a massive ice pack, a huge drifting field of ice that had unexpectedly come with the eastern sea current. Teams that left for Spitsbergen earlier have not reached Hornsund yet. They are either waiting in Longyearbyen or have given up all hope and decided to go back to Poland. The

---

1   A fjord in the southern part of Spitsbergen, where the Polar Station of the Polish Academy of Sciences is located, named after Stanislaw Siedlecki – a famous Polish polar explorer, and the Polar Station of Wroclaw ('Vrotslove') University.

sea has been blocked for three weeks already. That's most unusual. Such a situation has not been noted for many years. The organisers of our expedition considered the possibility of abandoning the whole journey, but finally we decided to take the risk. Everything is so changeable, especially the weather, wind and the ice-covered sea. You must only trust that it is going to change and take a turn for the better. However, our group of novices was not fully aware what we were going to miss if the expedition was cancelled. At that time we had not yet tasted the flavour of the Arctic, so we could not possibly long for it. It was just another interesting adventure. We could easily come to terms with the fact that we would miss that opportunity and that was because no bond or intimacy between us and that distant polar world had yet been created.

You feel the lack of something more acutely when it is familiar and close to you than the lack of something remote and undefined, although attractive. So my thoughts about the ice pack drew my attention not to our team but to a group of winter explorers who couldn't go back home as they were cut off from the world. The exchange of the winter staff was to take place three weeks ago. But they are still here locked behind the ice barrier in the fjord, deprived of their desire to go back home, to their daily lives, their family and different scenery. Everything is ready to return home – all bags, rucksacks, boxes and barrels have been packed. The rooms have been cleaned and emptied. Now they look lifeless and impersonal, as their occupants removed all their belongings from the shelves and walls. You must be ready when the ship comes into port, ready for a prompt boarding. But the ship is not coming. Imagine the ordeal of waiting when the voluntary parting with those you love becomes enforced. Especially, when after a year spent in the Arctic, in a small group of the same faces, you start to yearn for other surroundings. And then, all of a sudden, all your joy at the return is suspended and replaced with anxiety and concern. No one knows how long they will have to wait. The feeling of being powerless and having no influence on the developments is, first of all, what makes you so dejected. It makes your longing even deeper and more acute. The only thing you can do is to endure, wait and not lose your hope. Everything is changing in this world, so the situation here will also change, hopefully, for the better.

On both sides of this uncompromising ice-pack barrier there is the same faith that the adversities will pass and fate will be on our side again. There is the same hope in our eyes when we look at the unyielding mass of ice blocks. But will the captain take the decision to make yet another attempt to reach Hornsund? There are rumours that he might not. It could prove too risky in these conditions. Uncertainty lingers and then it prevails. Will we have to go back to the airport and finish this 'un-commenced' adventure in the Arctic? Suddenly, there is a decision.

We are setting off. We are leaving the harbour. All passengers of *Horizon II* are in the mood for adventure. We have challenged the destructive element of ice and are full of hope. As it turned out later, we were not the only ones.

The first hours of the voyage passed peacefully. The Greenland Sea was very favourable to us. In the distance we could see the shoreline showing faintly against the skyline. Somewhere there was the entrance to Hornsund fjord. However, the sea was getting denser. Small lumps of ice floating on the water became bigger and bigger, turning into ice blocks that started to fill up the whole sea. The ship was making its way more and more slowly. We could see a white line clearly visible on the sea surface at the fjord's mouth. It was getting bigger and bigger to become the ice barrier made up of thousands of big and small ice floes and blocks. It was sealing the way through. The ship was heading straight for it. Then came the first clash – the bow sailed into a narrow space between the ice floes and was patiently making it wider, wriggling its metal but fragile hull into it. Ponderously, inch by inch, with

Will the ship manage to break through the ice barriers?

4

the huge power of roaring engines, carefully like a blind man feeling his way around, the ship was entering the ice pack. Watching all this from the access hatches in the lower mess, we could only see the blue and white of the surrounding ice. Ice blocks were rising several metres high in the sea just within our reach. Our fascination was mixed with dismay. It was only then that we began to realise what it meant to challenge a massive ice pack. To make matters worse, we were in a small boat, which was not designed for a career as an ice-breaker. We observed with increasing anxiety how it struggled with the ice. We listened with terror to all cracks, creaks and thuds, sounds of combat with the hostile ice. The ice seemed to surround us like an enemy or a hunter holding its game at bay. Huge blocks of ice were crushing together, cracking and stacking, pushing and pressing with devastating power. They looked like monstrous silent giants that had elaborate shapes and had just emerged from the water. They were very dangerous, utterly unpredictable and contemptuous of our human fragility. At the same time they were dignified and beautiful – in their majesty. They were crowding around the boat as if they were curious what life onboard was like.

The track of keel water disappeared quickly. A narrow ice-free path behind us was immediately filled with ice floes. There was no way back. We were stuck in this

A Norwegian ice-breaker helps us to break through the ice pack.

ice desert. The moving power of the ship was getting weaker. It seemed we were not moving an inch forward. We were frozen in our tracks. We were trapped in the ice pack. What now? Is the history of *Fram*, Nansen's ship, going to be repeated? It may only be a matter of time before giant ice blocks crush a hull not strong enough to withstand such forces. It seems we have lost the battle. What will happen to us now? All this struck fear into our hearts.

But suddenly here comes help. Far behind us there is a looming picture of a ship. It is approaching us and slowly taking the shape of a massive ice-breaker, belonging to the Norwegian Coast Guard. We get hopeful again watching how it overtakes us and takes position in front of us. Then it starts to clear the way. The Norwegian ship elbowed its way through the crowd of ice giants letting us sail freely in its keel water. We followed our guide and carer obediently, like a little brother with infinite trust in an elder. The Norwegians led us out into the clear waters in the fjord. Afterwards nothing else stood in our way. I felt deep gratitude towards that unknown captain of the ice-breaker for his selfless decision of giving us a helping hand. It was the first important lesson of the Arctic moral code – you do not have to ask for help here. Everybody knows that without mutual support and helping each other you will not survive. Out of the harsh conditions and isolation of the Arctic environment, a natural habit of co-operation and co-responsibility is born. More than once I was to become convinced of this simple truth. Those who are incapable of giving spontaneous help and bearing responsibility for others doom themselves to social ostracism.

'We've just made contact with the Station of Polish Academy of Sciences in Hornsund. They are jubilant about our coming.' My friends have just descended from the captain's bridge where there is a radio communication centre.

'No wonder, poor boys have been waiting for this ship for ages. After so many months of isolation such bad luck at the end of their stay here.'

'It won't be long now,' Bartek (Bhartek) said. 'Tonight we'll celebrate breaking through the ice.'

'I see it's the first time you've been in Hornsund and you don't know its customs yet. You can forget about the party today. The unloading will start the moment we come in port and we are likely to work for two days or so.'

'Yes, yes … You celebrate when everything gets unloaded. At the same time it's the farewell party for the winter explorers.'

I listened attentively to my colleagues' conversation. Yes, there was a new world before me, with its own rules, laws and order. How do I become myself again in this new reality?

We were making for the port with no more obstacles in our way. The inside of the fjord was free from ice although from time to time you could spot some growlers

– single pieces of ice. The spacious sea was limited now to a stretch of water a couple of kilometres wide. On both sides there were more and more visible contours of the shores. Grey, rocky ridges, jagged from thousands of years of weathering and erosion by the sun, frost and wind. Wide valleys with glacier tongues. Ice fronts going softly towards the sea finished abruptly with precipitous cliffs. Ice blocks breaking off the glaciers and feeding ice floes with icebergs drifting on the water produced a landscape of grey and white tones. There was only a narrow greenbelt all along the shore on the port side. An intense green colour of tundra contrasted with the rest of this icy and rocky desert. Over it there was a steel-blue sky full of ragged clouds. That first view gave us some idea of extraordinary spaciousness of the Arctic scenery.

'This is our coast," explained Jasiu ('Yashiu') the head of our expedition and a regular in the Arctic, pointing to the distant greenbelt. It's the way you walk between the base, that is the Polar Station of Polish Academy of Sciences, and our university station called "Baranowka" (pronounced 'Bharhanoovka' – named after the famous

The grey and white landscape of the glacier foreland.

Polish climatologist and glaciologist Baranowski)'. 'Our coast' meant the Wroclaw ('Vrotslove') coast. I feel that our senior explorer put a strong emotional charge in this word. 'Ours' does not mean any formal appropriation of the territory or usurping any rights to this stretch of land. 'Ours' – because it was there that the history of the Wroclaw University Polar research was taking place. In the early 1970s this shore witnessed the transport of building materials for the construction of the Wroclaw University research station, Baranowka, which we were going to live in. It is this coast that was walked across so many times by the participants of subsequent Wroclaw expeditions. It is on this coast that the majority of their research was focused.

'Look! Just behind that headland there is Baranowka', it seemed as if his voice trembled and his eyes glazed over with tears. He was overcome by emotion as he was returning to the place he had known for years, of whose history he was a fellow architect, the spot where he had experienced both good and bad moments. All this creates an inextricable union between a man and a place. You feel strong emotions as the familiar shapes of the shores awaken memories that are always idealised by time and distance. For us, the 'freshmen' in Spitsbergen, the skyline had no significant meaning. Not yet. We tried to make out the rocky tip that obscured the view of our future home. We do not feel any of the bond or emotions you usually experience coming back to the place where you have been happy. Will we be happy here at all? We don't and can't possibly know yet. For the time being we felt the excitement of a new adventure. However, we were still far away from real friendship with this land.

I watched the shore slowly moving backwards. In two days' time we would be walking on it on our way to Baranowka – called also Werenhus ('Verenhus') in Norwegian. I prefer the latter as the Polish name sounds like 'ram's hut' in direct translation. Like an impartial observer I took notice of some details of the shoreline: the rocks having fancy shapes, mouths of several rivers and outlets of the valleys, bays – big and small, rocky slopes with carved deep gullies, massive talus cones at the foot of the mountains, cut through by periodic river beds. I wondered how I would perceive the same landscape in two months' time during my journey back home. Will the neutral and unfamiliar rocks, streams and peaks acquire new meanings? Subconsciously I knew what answer to expect. I was beginning to want to domesticate this unknown world. I wanted to regard it as 'my world'. But maybe it is just the strong wind that makes you choke on your words and gives you watery eyes.

Most of the ship's passengers have come out on deck. They are looking out for the Polar Station of Polish Academy of Sciences, our destination. It is difficult to notice as it is a low, ground-floor building, painted brown and green. This makes it melt perfectly into tundra.

Walking into the unknown.

Suddenly someone spots it. 'There it is!' It is hardly visible in the background. At least you can see clearly what is going on in the foreground on the waterside. There is a metal boathouse for storing boats and engines, called Banachowka ('Bhanahoovka') Boathouse (named after a famous Polish geographer – Banach, who started to build the boathouse). Just behind it, there is a unique petrol station, a neat row of snow-white fuel containers. We can see some small figures working busily by the boathouse. We can sense animation and excitement in this small waiting group. I imagine how happy they must be right now. They have just started to launch the first boat.

The people on deck get carried away by euphoria, too. The newcomers keep taking photos because everything is so new and fascinating, and you don't know if you will ever come back to this place again. Just in case all this should slip from your memory, you take as many photos as possible of this new world, to capture the precious moments.

The ship stops in the middle of the wide Polar Bear Bay, far away from the shore. We can hear the metallic clank of the cast anchor. All cargo – the people, luggage, food supplies for the winter explorers and building materials for the renovation of the station – is unloaded by means of small boats, dinghies or PTS boats. The last ones, a combination of an amphibian and a tank, deal easily with all kinds of heavy transport both on land and at sea. The ship cannot go any further into the bay due to numerous skerries – underwater rocks – which break the surface of the water. They make up a treacherous underwater maze that guards the access to the shore. Even if you steer a boat or dinghy of a shallow draught, it requires remarkable skill on the steersman's part. In addition to that, he/she needs to remember all the passages between the skerries.

Dangerous skerries and icebergs.

We are watching with admiration some dinghies approaching the ship. They manoeuvre with ease, zigzagging among invisible skerries and numerous ice growlers brought into the bay by the unfavourable wind. The steersmen had to spend the whole year in this tough environment, no wonder they are so skilled now. They were forced to learn how to live and survive in these hard conditions. The skill of navigation among skerries and growlers has been mastered simply out of necessity.

The first boat with the representation of the winter staff is approaching the ship. We can hear them cheering. We drop a rope ladder over the side. In no time the first winter explorers climb onto the deck.

'Welcome! Welcome!'

'At last you've come! We've been waiting for so many days.'

'Good to see you! How was your journey? How did you manage through the ice pack? We were really concerned for you as we listened to your radio reports during your passage.'

'How are you? How are you doing after the winter?'

'Hello, old man, how are things? You haven't aged a bit!'

The deck became a witness to one of the most extraordinary welcomes I have ever seen. All the people were flinging themselves into other people's arms, hugging each other, laughing and crying in turns. Some were chattering away while some remained silent, overwhelmed by emotions. But the power of their welcoming embrace was stronger than any words. The most amazing thing about this warm welcome was that we hardly knew one another. I had met those people for the first time in my life. I knew just one person in the group of winter explorers, namely Krzysiek ('Ksheeshek') – a climatologist from our Wroclaw Institute of Geography. Apart from him – nobody else. The other freshmen on the ship were in exactly the same situation. They did not know anybody. But it did not make any difference. Everyone greeted everyone else as if they had met their best friends, lost and found again, after many years of painful separation. On the one hand, we were strangers to one another, but on the other hand, we could not possibly be. Besides our two groups, that is, the winter explorers and the newly-arrived summer explorers, there were no other human beings within a radius of hundreds of kilometres. There was just the sea, mountains and icy space. In some situations the line between familiarity and unfamiliarity gets blurred very quickly. Sometimes it is just necessary. In that moment we all felt the same joy. We were happy that the ship had reached Hornsund. People were united by experiencing the same emotions and feelings, celebrating victory together – the victory over unfavourable elements and the happy ending of the ship in port. It was most unusual to watch that explosion of genuine emotions and tears of happiness shed by the winter explorers, released from their ice prison. It was even more amazing when you realised that they were all such strong and tough men. But they were so authentic in their joy at our meeting.

Once again the Arctic had shown us an utterly different dimension of a human meeting, the extent of magnified human relationships. The spontaneous euphoria of a meeting gives you a powerful strength and faith in other people. However, it does not always extend to daily life.

The unloading began. First people and luggage. Boats and dinghies go up and down the bay steering clear of ice and rocks in a most graceful way.

'Aga ('Ahgha'), Bartek, jump in! It's your turn now.' Jasiu takes charge of the transfer of our team to the shore. 'Watch out! I'll pass you your backpacks in a sec.'

After a couple of minutes we pull into shore. I step out onto the unstable gravel ground. There are pebbles all around, colourful, round, showing the beauty and abundance of rock formations in Spitsbergen. My first step on land. So here I am in Hornsund.

'Welcome to Hornsund.' Szymon's ('Sheemon') greeting echoes my thoughts. He is one of the winter staff supervising the unloading on the shore. 'Come, I'll show you to the base.'

We made for the building several hundred metres away.

I had imagined the wild Arctic in a slightly different way. The first impression of the surroundings of the station disappointed me. Marshy tundra and a wide muddy road damaged by heavy equipment – tractors and amphibians. Piles of scrap iron and rusty barrels waiting on the shore to be taken home. On the other side, a row of fuel containers. The neighbourhood reminded me more of an industrial landscape than the untouched scenery of the far North I expected to see.

We approached the station. Just before the entrance there was a flagpole with the Polish red and white flag fluttering in the air. In spite of my previous feelings of disgust and disappointment with the chaos around the station, I was overcome by quite a different feeling now. It was 'Polish House at the North Pole'. This patch of land was named by Polish Professor Stanislaw Siedlecki ('Sthaneeslove Shiedletsky'). He was one of the forerunners of polar research and one of those scientists who contributed greatly to the knowledge of the Arctic. The 'Polish House' was a stronghold of Polishness here in the middle of the ice and rock desert, a fact I suddenly understood looking at the Polish flag flying in the wind and quite unexpectedly I felt an overwhelming pride in my own nation. In everyday life you scarcely think about this, that you belong to a particular nationality. You are rarely proud of it. And suddenly, here, in this remote, desolate place, at the end of the earth, I can see my national banner. I would never have suspected before that I could be so patriotic. There were too many emotions for one day and it was not the end of it.

'Leave your backpacks in the hallway. The expedition leader will give you your rooms. I'm going to pick up the next teams.' Our guide led us to the very steps of the house. I went up onto the veranda. The first thing that drew my eyes was a red plate with a white inscription on it: 'The Stanislaw Siedlecki Polar Station of Polish Academy of Sciences in Hornsund'. An ordinary piece of metal, a few words, but sometimes it is just a tiny object that makes you appreciate the larger things.

'Hey, Aga, what's up? Is anything the matter?' Bartek did not share my fascination for that metal sheet. I don't blame him for that. On the whole, it was just a regular plate with the institution's name on it!

But I was looking far beyond it. I was rewinding my memories back to the beginning, when I was still a university student and a lot of my lecturers told fascinating stories about their adventures in Spitsbergen. The majority of the employees of our institute had been to Spitsbergen at least once. We were surrounded by the stories, even legends. We listened to them and absorbed every story and each picture of the Arctic shown on the old film slides. At that time, the Arctic world was as far away as some distant galaxy. Before my eyes stood the worn out pages of the books about the far North that I would read again and again, finding out more and more about the history of polar exploration, including the reports of the first Polish expeditions to Hornsund. And here just in front of me, there was this bright red plate, standing out and looking very real. Yes, Hornsund had ceased to be just the literary work or the colourful legend of our institute.

My presence here is a continuation of all the stories I have read or heard. I did not expect then that I would become a part of them. A very small, tiny one, but nonetheless a part of them. My disbelief blends with a great joy at making my dreams come true. With my head full of buzzing thoughts and mixed emotions I cross the threshold of the Polar Station. I feel the scent of wood and embrace the pleasant warmth of our Polish home at the North Pole.

The author.

2 Community

True People of the North spare no effort to bring help to others.
Jerzy Jasnorzewski, *Spitsbergen with no Retouch*

There was a flurry of activity both on the waters of the Polar Bear Bay and on the strip of land between the shore and the Polish Polar Station. In the middle of the bay, at a safe distance from the skerries (underwater rocks) there was the ship lying at anchor. Its colours – the white toned down with a wide blue stripe having a characteristic zigzag – blurred into the dazzling white of glacier tongues and the bluish glow of icebergs and growlers, as well as the light and dark-blue tones of the sky and water. Standing on the quay you could see a crane on the ship operating non-stop, unloading the subsequent batches of transported goods. Small boats and dinghies were toing and froing between the ship and the shore. They were moving swiftly and quietly, however, they were able to take only lighter cargo, people and luggage. The main transporting job was to be done by massive steel 'muscles' – two military amphibians, so-called PTS boats. They were roaring smoking monsters and rather slow in operation, but without them the unloading of the ship would be much harder and longer. There was no return to the old ways of the first Spitsbergen expeditions when they used a raft towed silently by boats. The inventions of contemporary civilisation definitely facilitate our lives greatly, especially in this whimsical and unpredictable polar environment; even if, on an everyday basis, we look with a scowl at all these noisy, tank-like vehicles that have ruined our previous idea of the Arctic being a virgin territory.

I am glad that the first strong emotion I could experience in Spitsbergen was this amazing feeling of community with others and the power given by belonging to a great 'polar family'. Of course, many times later I was to find out that like all families this one was not perfect either. It was no stranger to human petty-mindedness and meanness. Good moments were to mix with bad. But that was yet to come, not now. A good beginning is most important: this initial positive experience gave us strength and faith for later and let us turn a blind eye to all imperfections.

The ship was getting ready to depart. The boat that brought the last passengers was pushing off its broadside. A loud siren signalled the raising of the anchor. The ship's bow was turning slowly towards the mouth of the fjord and the open sea. It seemed all the passengers were gathered on deck watching the ship leave the bay. A similar group of keen observers assembled on the shore by Banachowka Boathouse. These were explorers who were staying in the Arctic for a couple of weeks or months, some of them for over a year. The people on the waterside watched the slow movement of the ship and silhouettes of those to whom they had just said goodbye.

Then follows an invariable ritual of farewell – a long-established tradition since the first Polish polar expeditions – someone on the land raises their hand and shoots a flare pistol. It goes up and flashes green in the sky between the ship and the shore. Here goes another one, and another one. It does not matter if it is your friends or strangers who are sailing away. It is not important who is staying. You are united by Spitsbergen time and space and a shared polar experience. The farewell flare or signal rocket is a symbol of solidarity between those who leave and those who stay. Once more you are overcome with this heartfelt emotion – the feeling of polar community.

Isn't it symptomatic, that you usually feel it when you are on the edge of some-thing? In this case, 'on the edge' of a welcome or farewell.

3 Tundra

No matter how hard I tried to take in the landscape around me, my efforts failed.
Maybe the beauty of the scenery was too great to encompass,
maybe the air was too crystal clear to comprehend anything,
no matter how much of it I inhaled.

Per Olof Sundman, *The Arctic Ocean*

'It's so colourful here!' The first moments spent on the shores of Hornsund were quite surprising for me. 'So many flowers!'

'So many' is obviously a relative notion, especially if you compare Hornsund tundra to Provence lavender fields, Dutch tulip plantations or luxuriant Polish meadows full of flowers. In this case the expression 'so many' could raise doubts. But we are in a place where the North Pole is just round the corner. Where the sun does not rise above the horizon for several months each year, and when it does, you can't see it anyway, because it does not often emerge from behind the clouds. In this context the multitude of colours we encountered on the shores of Hornsund was just amazing.

'The Arctic has revealed her new face, so far unfamiliar to us.' The boys from our team, who like me were here for the first time, expressed their admiration at colourful flowery shores.

It must have been really something if tough guys were moved at the sight of tiny plants. The intense greenery of the shores was thickly intertwined with clumps of purple saxifrages. It provided a pleasant diversion in a rather dull landscape that we could see on our way from Longyearbyen. For miles there had been just water, barren rocks, glaciers reaching the ends of the land or being suspended in mountain valleys and gravel pebbles on the beaches. All this in hues of grey and white. From the ship's deck the shores looked like a dead world, deprived of colours, sunken in lethargy, as hard as a rock, icy cold, and thus strange and unfriendly. And then, unexpectedly, we came across such an explosion of life and colour. We rejoiced over the regained diversity of the world.

'How come the Hornsund shores are so special and abundant in vegetation?' I couldn't see the reason for this intensity of life among the Arctic desert.

'That's very simple, look over there,' Andrzej ('Ahnjey') pointed at the high mountain chain rising close to the coast. 'Can you see it? Can you hear it?'

I did see and hear them. Thousands of birds were flocking between their homes on land and marine feeding grounds.

'This is the answer to the riddle. This is the explanation for the extraordinary luxuriance of tundra in Hornsund. In the clefts and rifts of the rocky slopes birds find an ideal habitat for nesting. Take for instance little auks; see how many of them are gathering here.'

The sky above us darkened for a while when one of the colonies of these birds flew overhead. They were small, looked like miniature flying penguins and were screeching at the top of their voices. It suddenly dawned on me.

'Natural fertiliser.' That's the mystery explained.

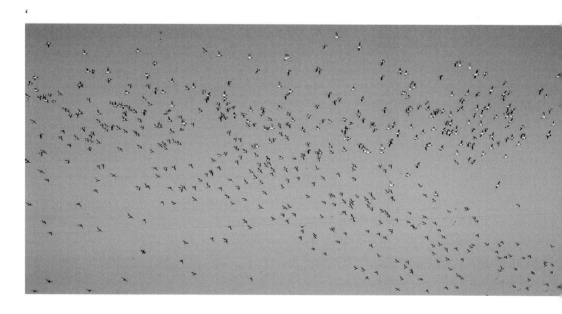

Count the little auks.

Yes, a very prosaic and down to earth reason. But the result looked undeniably beautiful. It was a narrow stretch of land between the mountains and the sea, which delighted the eye with vivid colours so different to the rest of the Arctic world.

We were lucky in our first encounter with Hornsund tundra. We came in the middle of the vegetation season. The tundra revealed its breathtaking beauty to us, as it was in full bloom. Various shades of the green dominated, from the lightest ones, such as willow green and yellowish green, through the bright greens, to more subdued green colours almost resembling brown.

In other places, vast areas of tundra looked like moorland due to numerous tufts of pink and purple saxifrages. While wandering in the tundra we discovered even more colours: white saxifrages, typical of this cold climate; mountain avens having eight delicate white petals, with light yellow stamens; yellow and white svalbard poppies with charming black inner sides of their small calyxes; white Arctic bell heather with beige tiny stripes, as well as intensely yellow flowers of sulphur buttercups. Unity of spring and summer. An outburst of extravagant colours. An explosion of life that has so little time to take delight in existence. After a few months of winter sleep and lifelessness, with no sun or warmth, the plants finally come out into the world. They grow quickly from bud to leaf to stay in full bloom as long as possible. It's as if the plants are saying:

> 'There is no time to lose. Let's cling to life, be greedy for the air, space and sunshine. It is our only chance to survive.' There is very little time ahead … and no-one knows if the summer weather will be favourable. Let's rush to live!'

But time flies, especially in the Arctic. Everything gets concentrated and the action of events is more intense than in the 'normal' world. Everything starts abruptly and ends abruptly. For a month I walked across tundra and enjoyed its summertime colours, and then suddenly I realised that the summer in tundra was gone. No warning signals had been given or harbingers of autumn had been seen. The majority of brightly coloured flowers disappeared overnight. I suddenly saw the palette of autumn colours. The tundra changed its 'robes'. Green and purple colours faded, the white ones grew dim. The autumn tones took their place – the tundra had grown red and golden. The trees started to change the colour of their foliage. I couldn't believe my eyes. The only 'trees' that we had in Hornsund were polar willows – tiny creeping plants, smaller than tall grass or some flowers. They started to take on different colours, their miniature leaves, being about half an inch long, which used to be a deep green shade, started to turn red, ginger, brown and golden. A real autumn. Only colourful lichen on the rocks remained as intensely coloured as they were before, as if the change of season did not relate to them.

'Since the autumn has already come, it's high time we went mushrooming,' someone suggested. In Poland it is a kind of a national pastime, everybody goes mushroom picking when the autumn sets in. The tundra did not fail us in this respect. Mushrooms bigger than the trees (polar trees, of course) popped up everywhere. Their caps and stems dominated the creeping 'branches' of the polar willows. It's difficult to say if they had been there all the time, or maybe they grew in a jiffy. I don't know. The month of August became the time for picking tundra mushrooms. Senior colleagues, experienced Spitsbergen regulars, assured us that we could relish any fruits of the tundra. All types of mushrooms were supposedly edible. We took a risk. We followed our national tradition of picking mushrooms, stringing them on a thread, hanging them over the oven and waiting for them to dry out. Then we cooked exquisite mushroom soup. And we all lived happily ever after.

Within two months in the tundra we would experience three seasons. An amazing condensation of time and events. A concentration of reality. A perfect lesson of life intensity. Don't put off anything. Don't wait until doomsday. Live your life to the full. The vegetation season is very short, even if it seems to us that it may last several dozen years.

Tundra trekking requires special skills.

'Watch out! Don't go there! It's tricky over the …' Too late … A seemingly stable ground covered with moss, which I had been treading on for an hour, suddenly caved in under my foot and sucked it in, straight into a swampy depth.

'Oh, no! My welly … Help me, please!' I was helplessly watching my wellington boot go lower and lower into the marshy mud. It was mire. I wasn't able to do anything. My up-to-the-knee wellies, which had been so practical thus far, were of no use here. I could watch the brim of the boot go under the treacherous bog moss. Splosh! I felt the unpleasant cold of water overflowing into it.

'How do I get out of here? Help me!'

The sight of the tricky ground with my own leg stuck in it made me quite panicky. I lost my usual nerve. I wasn't able to think clearly. Probably, if I hadn't had my heavy rucksack on, it would have been easier to free myself from the trap. But with a heavy load on my back it didn't seem feasible at all.

'Don't stay in one spot! Move or it'll get worse.' Yes, it's easy to give good advice when you are standing on the hard ground.

'You think I'm stuck here for fun?!' My helplessness caused irritation and impatience at otherwise useful suggestions.

'Keep your hair on! Try to move your body weight onto the other foot. Only then start pulling up your leg slowly.'

My companions outdid one another in giving pieces of advice, which were, unfortunately, quite hard to put into practice.

I leant over my trekking poles with all my strength. I blessed the fact that I had had a bright 'last-minute' idea to cram them into my backpack and take them for the expedition. I also blessed the moment when they finally stopped on some hard ground beneath, having been already swallowed by the bog up to one-third of their length. I moved my body weight onto my arms and other foot. Gradually, with a great effort, I started to pull my foot from the bog. I had not expected that friendly and nice-looking tundra would lure me into the treacherous greenery and softness of the moss carpet. Getting out of it was like slipping out of octopus tentacles. It was almost beyond my strength. I could only take my foot out of the welly, but the boot was still stuck in the clutches of the swamp. Finally, I gave up. I took out just my foot, leaving the boot inside. It was full of water anyway, so it didn't make any difference to my sock that I walked over the soaking wet moss.

At that moment, my colleagues ventured forth on a rescue mission to fish out the wellington boot. And they did it! Sitting on a dry edge of the mire I was looking at the spot where the boggy abyss wanted to pull me in. There was not a trace left. Not a sign. Maybe there was a small depression on the moss surface, but apart from that everything looked untouched. And very stable. For the rest of our way to Werenhus ('Verenhus') I could hear and feel rhythmic sploshing and squelching in my wet welly. I was lucky that we were not far away from the hut. I was happy with the regained ability to move both legs. Not to mention the recovered wellington. From that time on, I was rather suspicious of intensely green and lush areas of tundra.

There is one more danger you should know about, in this friendly, green and soft environment. This time it comes from the air. If you can see a figure of a man in the distance who is waving or throwing his arms or guns into the air, or whatever else he has at hand, such as trekking poles or a tripod stand, and it looks as if he is fighting with some invisible enemy – that is not a sign of madness, but an encounter with seabirds: skuas or terns. If you look hard, you will notice in the sky the shape of a small bird, which targets the man with its sharp beak, shoots like a bullet at him, and all this with the most peculiar determination. Then it retreats and returns to fight you from another direction. Defence becomes even more difficult when a pair of birds attack you. They fiercely protect their nest that contains eggs or babies. Terns are quicker and more agile in the air than skuas. They guard certain spots, while skuas control much wider areas.

Walking across the tundra on our route between the base and Werenhus we were exposed first of all to skuas. We learned by heart all vulnerable spots where we could be attacked by them. The shore was rather narrow there so we could not possibly walk around all their nesting places. We didn't even know exactly where they were. Both nests and nestlings' feathers merged perfectly with the background. You did not see them until they were right at your feet. The chaotic waving and throwing arms became our 'war dance' – an ever-present element of our trekking in tundra.

In spite of their dogged determination to attack us fiercely, the skuas won our hearts with their perfect acting skills. When their nest was still far away, despite losing their strength on fighting, they tried to trick us.

A bird comes right in front of us. She is limping and staggering, dragging her wing on the ground as if she wants to tell us how weak, ill, injured and inept she is. 'I'm easy prey. Follow me!' Continuing to limp and stagger, she consistently makes for a place in an opposite direction to her nesting spot. She is trying to draw the intruders away through this well-known behaviour. In this situation, you'd better be taken in by such tricks and follow the bird. You will avoid fierce attacks from the air. And when this sick bird, which was on the brink of collapse, miraculously returns to good health and all of a sudden soars up – it means that her nest is far behind you and you can continue walking.

There were real treasures hidden in the tundra, wonders of nature – natural masterpieces of art. The Earth is the greatest artist. There were patches of land with stony folds that lay in amazing regular circles. Elsewhere the rock debris created parallel stripes, reminding you of furrows in a potato field. Somewhere else the surface of the ground was covered with a network of irregular polygons that looked like honeycomb. Their edges were made of tiny stones, while the centre was filled with muddy loamy soil. The monotony of the slopes was broken by various cascades of miniature stairs, steps, terraces, as if someone was going to grow rice at the North Pole. The land was wrinkled here and formed folds and furrows, arrayed in curlicues – an astounding profusion of small forms and structures made of mud and stone. We admired stone circles that seemed to be arranged with great accuracy and attention to detail, maintaining the symmetry and regularity of the geometrical pattern. It was hard to believe that these were not made by human hand. It was ice, water and gravity that shaped them. They are Arctic artists – the abstractionists who use the alternate freezing and thawing of the ground as their artistic tools.

'Artistic' patterned ground.

4 Daily life

Nothing in this world is common and ordinary.
It is our inattention and disrespect that trivialize life.
We learned a very important lesson [in Spitsbergen]
of the great art of Not Becoming Accustomed.
Anyway, I am afraid that many of us are going to forget about it soon.
It is a skill that has to be practised.

(...) Everything that should happen will happen itself in its own due time.
(...) Peaceful settling in life, not measured by frantically passing hours,
not hastened by curiosity or passionate craving for shaping life the way we want it.

Jan Jozef Szczepanski, *The Polar Bear Bay*

One more short climb, one sharp bend, and we would see our destination from behind a rocky outcrop. We have been trekking for over five hours since we left the base. Our backpacks, with all our goods and chattels for this season, were quite heavy. They had been digging into our shoulders in a most unmerciful way. Even wellington boots started to chafe our feet.

'There it is! See the roof?' A small red rectangle stood out against grey and green tundra and rocks.

'It's so good to be home again!' We still had quite a walk to go, but we all livened up, and in spite of the tiredness we quickened our pace.

Werenhus ('Verenhus') or 'Baranowka' ('Bharanoovka'). In other words: The S. Baranowski Polish Polar Station belonging to the Institute of Geography and

Regional Development of Wroclaw ('Vrotslove') University. That is our house in the vast open spaces of the Arctic and I am going to cross its doorstep to spend my summer in Spitsbergen. We can now clearly hear the water of the rapid-flowing Brattegg river rushing down the rock step. It secures access to the Werenhus hut like a real moat. We walk over a narrow wooden footbridge above the waterfall. You can't risk this access during windy days. It's too dangerous, sometimes even impossible. You have to walk down to the river bed and go across the water. But just over this high-risk 'air bridge' there is a safe haven. This is a wooden house whose foundations are on the solid rock, with a nice veranda made from planks – where we immediately drop our heavy backpacks. We are not the first guests here this year. Not long before our arrival the winter explorers had been visiting. They treated Werenhus hut as an outing or weekend destination. Any time they needed to get away from the everyday monotony of the base, they split from their group and spent some time here – in solitude or in a narrow circle of friends, just for the sake of mental balance.

Werenhus welcomed us with a typical scent of wood and the sound of a creaking floor.

'I will organise the household chores and cleaning jobs for today.' Jasiu ('Yashiu') was a brilliant co-ordinator of our group made up of several people.

'Two strong boys will go now to Hyttevika to bring some of the staple diet products: loaves of bread, cheeses, cold meats, a couple of litres of milk, some margarine and tinned food. If you still have some room left in your rucksacks, you decide what else can be taken initially.'

Hyttevika was an old trappers' hut in the neighbourhood, which served that year as a port or depot where the barrels with our food supplies, spare clothes and equipment had been left. Now, step by step, we had to carry everything on our backs to the Werenhus half an hour away.

'Those who are staying will work in the larder. We must check "best before" dates of the products that were left over from previous seasons. We must sort out and put away things. Generally speaking, get it all sorted before fresh supplies come.' The head of our expedition kept on coordinating.

Each stay in the hus (hut) starts with tidying up. It is some kind of a phenomenon, because each season ends with tidying up too. Between the seasons nobody really lives here. From time to time, the winter explorers drop in for a day or two. Even though there is nothing much to tidy up, a certain ritual has been established. The first days of each expedition are dedicated to these activities. As if it was necessary to start a new chapter in the hut's life, to emphasise a new beginning by creating a new order in the space around us. Even if it comes down to moving a few packets of grits and rice onto another shelf, transferring tea bags from the larder to the kitchen, or stacking tins in the left corner of the stock room instead of the right corner. In the heat of the battle of unpacking, sorting, moving, ridding, putting away, you realise that it is not the cleaning that matters; it is the creation of a new reality. The reality that is established anew with each expedition. A kind of substitute for our own world – you must first give it a new form and structure to dwell within it safely. It's surprising how close it is from a prosaic activity of arranging tins, packages, cartons and jars to a metaphysical feeling of creating a new world order. It does not matter much that the world is confined to 14 square metres.

Our everyday life required that we should impose some order and rhythm on our daily activities. In the beginning it was rather 'disorder' that we experienced, not being accustomed to bright nights. We needed a couple of days to cure ourselves of our home habits; our bodies were completely disorientated by the constant daylight and did not feel the need for sleep. At first it was very difficult to switch to the new reality. The day and night merged into one. Waking up, you looked at your watch and you did not know if it was five a.m. or five p.m. The nights full of sunshine were totally unique and thrilling, especially to novices.

'You know, it's the first time I've done the soil survey and described the soil profile at midnight!' Czarek ('Tchaarek') expressed the excitement of all polar 'freshmen'. Each of us was fascinated by the possibility of non-stop field research unlimited by time, or to be precise, by darkness.

However, efficient daily functioning in a group required some regulation and normalisation into a 'day and night' routine. We gradually got used to the light of the night. It became natural. Finally, we stopped noticing it. The time for rest and sleep was determined according to 'theoretical night'. In practice we just covered the windows in the attic bedroom with a thick blanket to block out the sun. Sometimes, when it was raining continuously during the 'day' and the sun was shining at 'night', we had to readjust to a new rhythm in order to do any work at all. This happened for a week during one of our expeditions to Spitsbergen. We decided unanimously then that we should change our work and sleep schedule. So for a couple of days we set off to do field work at 10 p.m. in the sunshine. Relativity and conventionality of some matters turned out to be salutary in this case. At the same time we learned that the Arctic world is governed by the rules of nature. Our meticulous plans, intentions and schedules made and planned 'by the clock' and 'by the calendar' did not work here. Maybe such a system is efficient in the south, but definitely not in the north, at the North Pole. Here you must humbly submit yourself to the will of the weather. In spite of this knowledge, we insisted on bringing a new calendar every year, as if we wanted to maintain an appearance

Above: Hyttevika – the old trapper house and our deposit.

Below: Werenhus-Baranowka, the Polar Station of University of Wroclaw.

of our control over time. Every day, at midnight, we solemnly crossed out each passing day. One more ceremony in Werenhus of the everyday humdrum. And one more proof that it is extremely difficult to free ourselves from patterns set up in a different reality.

The household and cleaning regimes were repeated periodically over the whole stay in the hus. They did not have the broad scope and almost metaphysical depth of the initial operation, but they were purposeful.

'Well, lovelies, it's high time we dealt with this fishy business. 'Tis "tank action" today.' It was not a proposal you could vote against. It must be done. It's urgent and smelly. Literally. The emptying of the 'tank', which is our septic tank, luckily did not happen often. There was an unwritten rule that we use the toilet in the hut only if the weather was appalling. Otherwise, we went to the loo by the riverside but you mustn't forget to take a gun with you, just in case a bear wanted to take you by surprise in this open-air toilet.

'It's the best restroom I've ever seen. The natural "photo wallpaper" showing a panorama of 360°. Where else can you get such a view in the bathroom! The only snag is that the lavatory cistern is broken and it's flushing all the time …' I don't remember exactly which of the boys presented the advantages and disadvantages of our river toilet in such a vivid way.

During one of our expeditions, approximately once a week, we had a routine of 'cleaning the sausages'. It may sound strange, but it was an absolute necessity. One of the sponsors had generously presented us with supplies of cold meats and sausages, which suffered in transit, as they were kept in barrels on the ship for over two weeks. When they finally reached us, it turned out that they had developed a white greasy layer on the surface. The only solution was to wipe them regularly with water mixed with vinegar. It must have looked quite peculiar. If you could only see our small group sitting in front of the house, in front of a huge pile of sausages, brushing each piece of meat and wiping it with a tiny cloth. Putting our energy into it was some kind of Sisyphean labour. No matter how often we did that, after a couple of days they kept turning white on the surface again. And it did not help much that they were stored in a natural refrigerator, a pit dug in the moraine hill just behind the house. There were even pieces of huge ice blocks there that had broken off the glacier a long time ago, serving now as a fairly efficient ecological cold store.

Another big operation was the painting of Werenhus. We suspended all our field work and took advantage of the good weather. First, we arduously scraped off the old peeling paint, and then we industriously painted the walls with a new dark-green colour. The manufacturer had given it a very appropriate name: 'moss green'. It blended well with the background. To give everybody an equal chance to show off their artistic skills, parts of the walls were assigned to certain persons. We felt really satisfied and happy looking at our collective job done with our own hands. Later, when we were coming back home after many hours of field research, Werenhus welcomed us from far away with the intense colour of freshly painted walls.

However, at first, our meticulously planned painting was at risk. It almost failed because of a bear! Our paint tins along with the barrels of our supplies had been brought by the ship earlier and unloaded in the port at Hyttevika. When we reached the place a few days later, some of the tins were completely trampled and crushed. On the grass all around them there were clearly visible green footprints or rather 'paw prints'. We knew the culprit immediately. We had heard stories about bears having washing powder for lunch, draining barrels of sunflower oil, nibbling at plastic containers, not to mention trampling and tearing, even 'trying on' one explorer's Sunday best clothes: but savouring the paint? It turned out that the basis for the paint was fish oil, which protects items perfectly well from going rusty. In case of doubt the bear always follows his nose, which did not fail him this time either. Fortunately, he did not take a fancy to this kind of 'food', and some tins remained intact. But it was not enough to paint the whole hut. However, all was not yet lost, as one member of our team was going to join us at some time later and was still at home. We quickly called for 'emergency action', and after a couple of weeks a new delivery of the paint arrived from our home country. This time we did not linger a moment but got down to work instantly. The green prints of the bear's paws could be seen on the grass in front of Hyttevika hut for a long time after the crime had been committed – an impressive indication of the quality and resilience of the paint product!

All those cleaning, household and sanitary operations requiring team work happened once in a while. They were some kind of an interlude and variety in our everyday activities. Daily life was quite ordinary – of course to the extent of the Arctic ordinariness. First the field work, which used up most of our time and energy, then compilation of collected data in the cosy atmosphere of Werenhus. Poring over our books or notes in the cloudy August evenings, we would often have to turn on the lights – as the polar day was coming to an end and the sun was getting lower and lower on the horizon. Sometimes, to create a 'romantic' atmosphere, we would light candles and have a candlelit dinner. Each day, one of the teams (and we used to operate in pairs, for security reasons) would volunteer for cooking duty in the kitchen to prepare dinner for others. It was so nice to come back home after the whole day spent in the field and find hot soup on the table … followed by the second course and dessert. The best chef of all and master of the culinary art was Jasiu. The dishes made by him were not only delicious and varied but also served in a most elegant way. Sitting at the table you had the impression that you were in a luxurious restaurant in one of the European capitals, definitely not in the polar desert.

I liked staying in Werenhus on my own, when everybody else had dispersed to their field stands. The hut was filled then with such peace and quiet. In those moments I could just delight in my presence in that place. In anticipation of my companions' return, usually tired and freezing, I enjoyed doing all the household

Drying wet clothes, boots and… mushrooms – the kitchen in Werenhus.

chores, such as peeling potatoes, cooking, washing up or sweeping the floor, so boring and monotonous in 'normal' life, but gaining a new meaning here. Especially when you could see your friends' faces cheering up at the sight of hot food.

Our daily life in Werenhus consisted of the usual activities, but each of them, cooking, washing or cleaning became, in these Arctic conditions, the celebration of a certain moment. Each task to be done, no matter how trivial it would be, became the most important thing at a given moment in time. The most distinctive feature of everyday life in the Arctic is its lack of haste and hurry. But this understanding came later. Our life in Werenhus went on as if in slow motion. In fact, it was a natural pace of life, as contrasted to the continuous rush of hard-pressed people 'in the South'. To most of us, who lived in such a way in our usual conditions back at home, it seemed that the world slowed down. But life went on, not being rushed by anything. It made us attentive and aware of every moment and experience, and allowed us to enjoy every job we did. It may sound banal perhaps, but it is very simple. Think of the depth of tranquillity you can experience sitting on a bench, in front of a hut, with a mug of hot tea in your hand, when you look at the vast Arctic space toward the horizon, the skyline of jagged mountains at one side, and the dark line of the sea at the other side. Or imagine your peace of mind when you spend your time in a team of people who get on well together, enjoy working and spending free time together, staying awake throughout the light polar nights, chattering away at the kitchen table.

It was there in the combined kitchen and living room, next to the stove, that our social life concentrated. We had our meals there. We lavishly celebrated birthdays and name days of our team members, watched films, looked at photographs on the laptop and had lengthy conversations and 'panel discussions'. It was in that place where we were challenged by extremely difficult crosswords brought by Czarek during one of the expeditions. It was there that we practised our singing skills and other talents, and came up with all sorts of strange but ingenious ideas. At that kitchen table we sampled so called 'antidepressant' substances such as home-made Werenhus Reindeer Vodka, Cladonia Booze (in other words Reindeer Lichen Vodka) and Brattegg Vodka. They were all 'top quality' beverages and so they required proper labelling. Being suddenly seized by poetic inspiration we created rhymed labels for all of them. In later seasons the Lemon Cordial – in Polish: Cytrynowka ('Tseetree-noovka') – took over the market. This fine liqueur produced by our fellow hydro-geologists made Werenhus famous in the whole Hornsund. On the walls of our dining room, in the framed old photographs, we could see the faces of our predeces-sors – the precursors of polar research in the area of today's Werenhus, i.e. Stanislaw Baranowski ('Sthaneeslove Bharanovsky') after whom Baranowka hut was named, and Alfred Jahn ('Yahn') – a famous professor of Wroclaw University. They are smiling indulgently, looking at our life in Werenhus. They both did a lot of research in the Arctic. Their figures in the black-and-white photographs remind us of our responsibility and significance of our presence in this place.

My first encounter with a polar bear also happened when we were sitting at the Werenhus table. We were having a snack, talking … when suddenly the window, just by the table, was filled with a huge white mass. A bear! His body took up the whole width of the window. He was peeping into our house with a great curiosity as if he wanted to find out what was going on in that little hut. We were just a thin wall and a window pane apart. The majority of people in the hut were in Spitsbergen for the first time, so they all reacted in a very emotional way. However, our actions were more proactive. We all jumped to our feet and grabbed whatever weapons we could from the kitchen cupboards: pots, lids, ladles and frying pans. They all work quite well when you need to scare off a bear. Making a horrible noise with this gear we all got out of the house. Everybody except for Bartek ('Bhartek') who kept his cool and grabbed his camera instead of a saucepan. Thanks to him we could all enjoy a photograph of our first polar bear – posing for his portrait in the frame of the window.

Nothing important or remarkable seems to happen in daily life. It is strange that living so close to the North Pole, surrounded by such unique nature, we were consumed by down-to-earth tasks, such as renovating, cooking or washing. But the time spent at Werenhus was by no means ordinary. We were starting to understand the notion of 'everyday life'. We were gradually discovering that the most essential thing is *being*, in this place and at this time. Obviously our plans, intentions and work were important too, but the essence of experiencing the Arctic is much deeper and greater than anything we could ever produce or create. The life itself is the essence, absorbing it with all your senses and relishing it day after day – even in the most ordinary activity. Attention paid to every minute reveals the extraordinary richness of everyday life and a simple joy of existence.

I discovered this truth while cruising in a small boat on the Greenland Sea. From the diary of my first stay in Spitsbergen:

> *It is not always easy to be calm and serene in life. But we must learn how to feel its rhythm, not to do anything forcefully and against ourselves – and the peace will come on its own.*

It is like going by boat on the sea. You must submit yourself to the rhythm of the sea, go up and down with the waves, trust your boat and the steersman, and go on. Sitting in the bow you feel the wind on your face and drops of water splashing against the boat. You sense their wet freshness and salty taste on your lips. Salt on your face and in your hair. You squint your eyes. Your cheeks and eyelids are basking in the sun's warm golden rays. Its warmth fills you as you head towards its golden disc hanging low on the horizon. It is gilding the icebergs and painting the sea depths blue. The abyss is right beneath you. Around you – the fantastically shaped ice blocks and dark shades of skerries. I enjoy this incredible moment, among ice floes, in the far North, on a sunny day. My thoughts are filled with space, sea and wind. I let the boat carry me over and down the waves. I fly over the water with seabirds and salty wind – my brothers.

You must let the waves carry you and don't worry too much about the future, how big or strong the next wave may be … You must surrender to it and make towards the sun. You must entrust yourself to the steersman entirely…

During one of the summer seasons a TV crew arrived at the Polar Station of the Polish Academy of Sciences in Hornsund. I happened to be in the base then. There was a general excitement and commotion. 'They are going to make a film about Polish polar explorers! It's not just any short programme.' The topic of polar research has become very newsworthy in recent years. So it was an ideal subject. For a few days, the film director and camera crew took people to make short films in the field and in the labs. Each explorer representing a particular scientific area was supposed to talk about what kind of research they were doing in Spitsbergen.

'You have five minutes to elaborate on it. Please, do not use any difficult words or expressions. Everything must be clear to the common man and amateurs. Preferably, you start with a surprise or some sensational news, and continue like that. Then the excitement should grow – like in Hitchcock's films. Remember, it is action and shock that matters.'

The film director was giving me detailed guidelines when we were still off camera. But I felt mutiny inside me. It was a big mistake. It was ludicrous! These teams of reporters and journalists working for TV, press or radio come over to Spitsbergen in a hurry, for a couple of days, because they are so pressed for time. And being so keyed up they want to discover the essence of the Arctic, looking only for superficial impressions. But what is absolutely indispensable? They need some sensation.

They don't get it: that the most important things in the Arctic happen in daily life, filled with seemingly ordinary activities. Just being there is the essence. Relishing precious moments. The slow pace of life. Peace and quiet. Vast space. Friendship and helpful people around you. How unlike the media. It is doubtful if the media would get interested in such things at all. After all, there is really nothing to talk about, is there?

5 Radio

Here [in the Arctic] each meeting may be a request for help or for passing an urgent message.
Turning your back on somebody here is a much more serious issue
than just a manifestation of bad manners.

Jan Jozef Szczepanski, *The Polar Bear Bay*

'Base, base, Werenhus ('Verenhus') is calling,' the microphone of the radio set is whirring a bit when we try to get in touch with the base, the Polar Station of the Polish Academy of Sciences 16 kilometres away.

'Werenhus, Werenhus, this is base speaking. Let's go over "14", you could usually tell after the sound of the voice which person answered the call, and thus was on radio duty in the base. Sometimes, however, the interference of the radio signal was so strong that you couldn't even recognise the voice of a person well known to you. But the most important thing was to understand each other well, pass a message or obtain information.

'I'm on "14"', I reply, having switched a small knob in Werenhus radio set onto channel 14. That particular channel was used for conversations. Number 16 was treated as a security channel and was used only for initial or general calling out.

This is the way the majority of Hornsund conversations start. The names of places and numbers may change but the scheme stays the same. It is like a magic formula, which helps you to conjure a person you want to make contact with. A certain spell that makes you feel the presence of other people, even in the most remote and solitary places on Earth. It is just a beam of electro-magnetic waves, you may say, but it does give you a sense of security: 'I am not alone. I am heard and I listen. I transmit and receive messages. I broadcast.'

Radio transmission is the basis of communication in the Arctic world. The base has all the latest technological developments, such as the internet or a satellite phone, but all other regional stations and people doing field work must rely on more or less reliable portable radio transmitters. It happens that electric discharges come, or some obstacles arise in the terrain formation. The radio transmitter crackles, whirs or breaks off for good. We are cut off from the world. We must firmly believe that nothing bad is going to happen to us and we will come back within the signal range.

'OK, thanks. That's all for now,' the messages have been relayed and arrangements confirmed. Radio communication teaches you how to formulate your thoughts and utterances clearly and concisely, how to express your needs or ask questions in the most understandable way. You must be logical and precise. You shouldn't muddy the waters.

'OK, over and out. I'm back to "16".'

We close channel 14 – the conversation channel. We maintain a continuous radio watch on '16'. We are waiting for further signals and we are ready to bring help to those whose voices will reach us even from far away.

'We'll keep in contact.' We repeat it like a mantra in our daily lives and never think of its significance. Why should we? In today's era of the internet, emails or mobile phones what else can be easier than 'staying in contact'. It seems so obvious. However, the Arctic teaches us to discover its sense anew. In the far North this meaning is not so explicit or obvious any longer. There is no internet in Werenhus. The mobile phones do not work. We have had the satellite phone for a short time now but its resources are limited. It cannot be used for chatting with your family or friends. It is kept in Werenhus primarily for safety reasons, in case we need to call for help. From this communication desert we set off on a previously planned, long journey to the base, in order to make just a short phone call to relatives or friends. The occasion may be your brother's birthday, wife's name day or son's important examination. A couple of hours of marching back to civilisation in the base, very often in the drizzle or fog, just for the sake of a few minutes of a telephone conversation. It is an enormous physical effort and logistical challenge. We undertake it to convey one of the most important messages: 'I am with you. I think about you. I remember you.' We just want to 'keep in contact'. In this context the phrase takes on a whole new dimension.

At first, I couldn't get used to the radio communication at all. Actually, I wasn't accustomed to anything in Spitsbergen. The first days in Werenhus were hard for me.

The world around me was entirely new and it seemed strange. I had to learn it bit by bit and organise it – not only by putting my belongings on the shelves. First of all, I had to get my thoughts in order. Work in the new field conditions, new washing and cooking facilities, and worst of all going to the riverside loo with a gun on my arm. A group of new people around me, who were only beginning to make friends with one another, operate together and define their position in a team. In addition to that, constant drizzle, mist and damp. The weather definitely did not help me in my first days in the Arctic. I was down in the dumps. I started to think that all this was beyond my capabilities. Maybe I wasn't cut out for this place. Everything was so difficult or demanding. I felt bad, that I was too weak to live in such conditions.

I am not sure how things would have worked out if it had not been for one particular event that became a landmark in my Arctic life. And that involved the radio. The four of us had been living in Werenhus for three days already. Soon our fifth participant, one more girl, Anka ('Ahnka'), was supposed to arrive with a group of Czech speleologists. It was late afternoon and we had just returned home from the field. We were soaking wet as it had been drizzling since the early morning. We were getting dry in the kitchen when a soft humming of the radio was suddenly broken by a call directed to us.

'Werenhus, Werenhus. Base is calling.'

'Base, base. This is Werenhus. 14?'

'Yes, 14,' a few seconds for a change of channels and we are listening to the message from the base.

'We've just got a message from the Czechs and your friend Anka. They are on the *Eltanin* yacht and should reach Hornsund in two hours. But they can't go into Nottinghambukta port. The tide is out and steering around the skerries would be too dangerous. They're going to moor at Hyttevika. The Czechs are asking you for help. Could some of you from Werenhus go there and give them a hand with unloading? They've got loads of luggage and equipment. And you know, in this weather the unloading action should be done as soon as possible. Over.'

'Sure, no problem. We'll set out in a moment.'

'All right, good luck to you. Over and out, 16.'

With no grumbling at all, Bartek ('Bhartek'), Czarek ('Tchaarek') and Jasiu ('Yashiu') started getting ready to go out. I was obviously getting ready, too. I wanted to contribute to this team effort.

'Wait a sec, we can't all go. Somebody has to stay and guard the hus. One moment of distraction and we'll end up with a polar bear sitting at our table in the hut … And the stove, it must be tended too.'

Listening to the men's line of reasoning – quite logical on the one hand – I already knew what they were up to.

'Aga ('Ahgha'), you'd better stay at home. You won't be much use with heavy load, but in the hus you'll do a great job. And we'll need somebody to be alert and listen to the radio. We'll take our walkie-talkies and be in touch.'

I had to admit they were right, their arguments were rational, but in my heart of hearts I was hurt. 'It's all because I am a woman. They think I can't do anything right apart from sitting at home. Why can't I prove that I am strong too and able to do hard physical work?!' Luckily, those negative emotions soon give way to more positive ones: 'I am responsible for the house, for the fire and warmth. They'll be back in a couple of hours and it is exactly what they are going to need. I can't fail them.' From this perspective, my staying in the hus – against which I was initially so rebellious – turned into a kind of special mission. It is amazing how the same prosaic fact can be interpreted in different ways and evoke completely contrasting emotions. But finally, it is me who chooses the interpretation. I have chosen 'mission'. It is better than the attitude: 'Women are of no use, they should stay at home.'

It took quite a while for the team to set off for Hyttevika. They went out and walked across the tundra in their wellington boots, zipped-up anoraks, with the hoods pulled low over their eyes, struggling with the wind and drizzle. Through the kitchen window I could still see their figures getting smaller and smaller until they disappeared behind the rocks at the foot of Gullichsenfjellet. I was left all alone for the first time since I came to Spitsbergen. In the first few days there were people all around me at all times – crowds in the base and our small group in Werenhus. I was constantly accompanied by someone. Now I was on my own. Just me and the new world that was so hard to make friends with, in which I just couldn't pull myself together. Looking after the hus, feeding the fire, short-wave listening duty. Nothing special, but in that place, in that particular moment, there wasn't anything more important. Once more, the far North perspective taught me to appreciate apparently unimportant things and see them in a different light. The sense of responsibility binds us to the world and the people for whom we are responsible. And maybe such commitment is just one more unnecessary burden in our lives? One more impediment? On the contrary. Without responsibility our existence lacks depth and full dimension. It gives sense to our life; being responsible for something, for someone, means that we are needed. And who of us does not feel inside this natural human longing for being needed by others? Deep in our hearts we want to feel the relation between our life and the surrounding reality and lives of other people. Even if we put on masks of indifference and detachment. Responsibility is a vital element of cultivating such relationship.

Those long hours I spent on my own in Werenhus allowed me to feel and understand my true presence in that world. With every passing hour, each piece of coal put into the stove, every crackle made by the radio – I felt more and more at home. While waiting for my old and new companions to arrive I got rid of the anxiety and feeling of uneasiness I'd experienced so far. I was in charge, I had a task to fulfil, a mission to accomplish. The world and the people needed me. When you become aware of this there is no more room for the feeling of alienation.

The first few hours after the boys' departure went by peacefully. In the beginning, I had to get over my fear of being left all alone. My biggest worry was what would happen if a white quadruped friend wanted to pay me a visit? But soon I got down to my work. I had quite a lot of field notes to complete so I spread all my maps and papers on the table, in the kitchen of course, next to the radio and the stove, which I was going to check systematically. Beside the papers I put some bullets on the table and brought the gun from the hallway to hang by the door in the kitchen. I wanted to have it close at hand, just to be on the safe side.

'Werenhus, Werenhus, *Eltanin* is calling.' Despite crackling you could hear a distinct Czech accent.

Up until this moment it was always one of the boys who operated the radio. Now there was nobody else except me to do that. A moment of panic – where do I pick it up, which button to press, which knob should I use to minimise the whirring, where is '14'?!

'*Eltanin, Eltanin*, this is Werenhus. Let's switch to 14.' I heard my own voice, but it was such a strange and serious voice. It was the first time in my life I had talked on the radio in such a situation.

'Fourteen. We have a delay. The waves at the fjord's mouth made it very hard for us. But we're almost reaching Hyttevika. Is somebody from Werenhus coming to help us? We could do with an extra pair of hands.' Pepa, the Czech, was speaking Polish fluently, adding one or two Czech words now and then.

'Don't you worry about that. They left a long time ago. Three strong men. They must be already waiting for you at Hyttevika.'

'That's good. Thanks a million! You must be Agnieszka ('Ahgnyeshka'). Anka told me about you.'

'Yeah, that's me. I'm guarding the hus and waiting for you with some tea.'

'That's very nice of you. And one more thing. Can you contact the base, please, and let them know we have a delay. Cheers!'

And so it began. My night-talks on the radio. First, exchanging information with the base, then with Pepa, the base and Pepa again. I was slowly getting accustomed to this new means of communication. Werenhus became some kind of an intermediate transceiver station between the base and Hyttevika. It was impossible for them to make a direct contact. The short-wave walkie-talkies were out of range. In this way

I became the missing link in transmission. My listening out for the radio was most necessary and useful to others. It made sense. I enjoyed my new role.

Midnight was nearing, but the horizon, where I should see a group coming from Hyttevika, was still empty. I looked at it regularly and was beginning to worry. 'What's taking them so long? It's been quite a long time since the first conversation with Pepa.' I tried to call Hyttevika, but nobody responded. They probably had switched off their walkie-talkie. There was no contact. The only thing I could do was to wait patiently, control my growing anxiety and see to the fire. I put the kettle on for tea. They could be coming back at any moment.

Gradually, sleep was taking hold of me. I was getting more and more tired. 'But I can't possibly fall asleep. I must be on my guard! I can't fail them.' My head was constantly nodding. I couldn't keep my eyes open. Finally, I decided to have a nap, but in the kitchen, with my ear by the radio. I brought my sleeping bag from the attic bedroom and I spread my body over a narrow kitchen bench. It was definitely more useful for sitting. But then I did not mind that at all. I set the alarm clock for an hour: I decided to feed the fire at hourly intervals. I don't remember now how many times during that night I got up and put the next pieces of coal into the stove. I had no experience to tell if the fire that was burning in the stove was sufficient to last for the following hour. I had no idea how many bits of coal I should add to maintain a certain temperature. Living in a block of flats with a municipal central heating does not enrich your knowledge of tending the stoves. I had a dim memory of a coal stove that stood in my family house many years ago. But this vague reminiscence from my childhood did not translate into practice. However, that night I did my best to complete that fast course in stove operation and tried to understand its workings! I was so concerned about the possibility of putting it out that I would put into it twice as much as was necessary. I was the guardian of the hus fire, I could not possibly let it go out.

It was only in the early morning that I saw some small figures against the rocky horizon. The first three people were burdened with huge backpacks, the next two followed them. Their shapes were getting bigger and bigger as they approached the hut. But it was still impossible to recognise who was who at a distance, especially as I did not know the Czech team.

'Here they come!' The sight of the small points moving towards Werenhus made me feel utter joy. And relief. As if my waiting for them had lasted for months, not for a couple of hours. Since the kettle had boiled dry I put it on again.

At last I heard the usual creak of the door. After a moment Bartek and Czarek entered the kitchen, dropping huge heavy rucksacks filled with food supplies onto the bench.

But instead of 'hello' I heard, 'It's scorching hot in here! A real sauna or Turkish bath.' My 'mission' to keep up the fire was completely underrated. My efforts and the fact that I got up every hour to tend the stove were unappreciated.

'It's around 40°C in the hut,' the boys wouldn't stop with their comments.

It was a fact. When I climbed into the attic, the heat was unbearable. Downstairs in the kitchen you didn't feel the temperature was so high. We had to open all the windows wide. 'Well, I thought, it takes some practice to become a perfect Vestal virgin.[2] After all, Rome was not built in a day.' However, hot tea was appreciated by everybody, as they were all frozen. I was so happy that I could give them that tea, that they did not come back to a cold empty hut but to their home, where somebody was waiting for them. Their home, full of warmth, even if the temperature surpassed all expectations.

After that night-long watch spent by the radio and stove I gained something important for myself. I tamed a new reality. I found my place in it. I grew attached to it, very much. When we become responsible for something it stays within us forever. Since that very moment I have not thought about Werenhus in any other way than 'my Arctic home'. The dilemmas and predicaments of the first days vanished into thin air.

Radio accompanied us in many other situations. We tried to have it switched on all the time to maintain a kind of a radio watch. However, that was only possible in Werenhus, when we had electric power 'in abundance'. Apart from a generator there used to be two homemade power stations, wind and water powered, constructed by Szymon ('Sheemon'). Sometime later our electric sources were limited only to the generator, and portions of energy had to be limited. The radio was silent then. We only made appointments with the base to get in contact at certain hours and switched on the radio to report to them. Otherwise there was silence. But when we had plenty of electric energy, we could listen to all kinds of messages travelling across the ether. They were like radio programmes to us. Radio chatter of the ships passing our shores, messages from the ships to the base and from the base to the ships, were a kind of entertainment in Werenhus, cut off from civilisation. We would often listen to snatches of conversations, most often in Polish, Norwegian, Russian and English and tried to guess what was going on in the wide world just round the corner. The world that reached us by means of invisible waves, and materialised in the form of

---

2   In ancient Rome Vestal virgins were responsible for maintaining the sacred fire in the temple of Vesta, the goddess of the hearth.

sounds, that sometimes were barely audible in the crackling and humming of our old run-down radio set. Some messages coming from distant seas remained a mystery forever, especially if we could hear only one voice.

'What type of a ship is it? What language? Did you get who they were calling out?' By means of the radio we soaked up all the latest bits of information, and had a chance to exercise our imagination as well as our ability for intellectual speculation.

First of all, radio communication, which was one of the most important Spitsbergen discoveries for me, was a powerful means of creating links and bonds between people in desolate places where other means of communication failed. Being out of range of mobile phones or the internet, on the high seas or in remote research stations all over the world, we never cease to need contact with other people. It is not only in the case of an emergency when you have to call for help to save somebody's life. But also in everyday situations, when an equally important message is sent: 'I am alive, everything's OK, how are you?' 'Who are you?' 'Where are you heading on your ship?' The conversations travel across the boundless waters of the ocean linking tiny islands of our human existence. We are not alone. We send our messages and listen out for a response. We are a link in a great chain of interpersonal human communication.

I have always wondered at the fact that the theme of radio runs through all notes and accounts of previous polar expeditions. For the first Polish polar explorers, radio communication was the only way to remain in contact with the world, apart from traditional post services that usually had a delay of a couple of months. During the first Polish expedition that spent the winter in the Arctic (in the year 1957–58) there were special radio programmes broadcast from Warsaw, once a week, to remain in contact with the explorers and their families. They were famous broadcasts run by the journalist Czeslaw Nowicki ('Tscheslove Noveetsky'): 'Hello Spitsbergen! Hello Hornsund! Good Evening, Dear Friends!' There is no such need today. In the era of the internet we are in a more privileged situation. However, as it turns out, radio communication has not yet lost its power.

6 Visitors

This kindness was not pretended. How else can you treat another human being in the Arctic than in a friendly way? (...) Isn't it obvious that this cold remote territory must be the land of reconciliation, where we can afford to be just human.

Jan Jozef Szczepanski, *The Polar Bear Bay*

The Arctic is most often associated with an endless white space or the ice-cold, desolate desert. It is perceived as a hostile and inhospitable emptiness, where the presence of a human seems preposterous or against basic principles. Is there any other place than a desert where you can feel more acutely the solitude when surrounded by nothing but ice and rock and unable to reach the horizon hovering in the translucent air?

But there is more to the Arctic world than we expect. It has some other nature, too. Probably nowhere else can you find life in such a condensed form. The 'population density' per one square metre of floor surface in the small wooden shelters (scientific stations) soars in the summer season, and the huts are throbbing with life. This is the astonishing paradox of this ice-covered land, where extremes are commonplace, where the emptiness of solitude evolves imperceptibly into an excess of the physical presence of other people. We do need others around us. We draw our strength from community, from being a part of a bigger entity. But at the same time, we have to stray from the group to define our own boundaries, to maintain our internal integrity. These contradictory needs, which we know so well from our daily lives, become magnified in the Arctic, they swell up to the point of maximum endurance and then they explode in the most unexpected way. Living for a couple of weeks or months in a small group of people confined to a small space means not only scientific research contributing to the world's knowledge but also, and maybe first of all (whether we like it or not), a great psychological experiment. In extreme conditions, struggling in turn with solitude then with crowded living in confined spaces we react in ways we would have never anticipated.

Perhaps this undesigned experiment involving our unaware participation will bring more into our lives than all the research results, however ground-breaking, that may be published in scientific magazines.

'Werenhus, Werenhus, this is base. Over.' A creaking voice speaking from the radio stirred us from the evening apathy.

The day's weather was very favourable, so we all spent a very long and intensive day on the field work. We were dead tired. The radio calling out of our hut livened us up. 'What message do they have for us?' It was a kind of surprise and entertainment at the same time. Sometimes even a basic announcement added variety to our monotonous life which was filled with the same activities.

'Yes, this is Werenhus. Let's switch to 14.'

'Hey, Wroclaw ('Vrotslove') guys, would you like to come to the base this Saturday? We are going to celebrate Christophers' name days – we have plenty of them at the base this year, as many as three,' Marek ('Mharek') laughed heartily, 'so we are preparing a party worthy of the occasion. You are very welcome, too. Will you come?'

We looked at one another with full approval. It went without saying.

'Of course, we will! We also have one Christopher and will include him in the group of "name-day boys". And we will join the party.' Heniu ('Heanyu') immediately expressed the enthusiasm of our whole group.

'That's superb! See you on Saturday then. By the way, don't forget to bring your swimming costumes 'cause we are going to a tropical beach to swim,' the last bit sounded quite intriguing, 'For volunteers, of course,' Marek added quickly, as if afraid that the prospect of bathing in the Greenland Sea may put us off going.

'The beach?! Actually, there is a beach all along the shore, full of gravel pebbles, but a tropical one? Hmm, what on earth are they up to?' There is no other way but to go and see it for ourselves.

There were still a few days left until Saturday's expedition to the base, but we were beginning to prepare for it. And we were looking forward to it. The trip to the base, just 16 kilometres away, was always some kind of a celebration because it was done so rarely. We focused, first of all, on our field work in the vicinity of Werenhus. Our timetable was demanding, and there was always a risk of lagging behind schedule because of unfavourable weather. So in fact, we couldn't afford too much free time just for chilling out or sociable walks, especially as covering this apparently short distance was no easy task. It always took several hours, either along the shore, walking on unstable pebbles, or across the tundra, where your feet sank deep, sometimes up to your knees, in the wet moss and peat. Such circumstances did not facilitate or speed up the journey. As a result, the trip assumed the proportions of a real 'expedition'. However, from time to time, each of us needed that. Not for the sake of walking, we had plenty of that every day. We spent long hours doing strenuous field work. We needed that to change our surroundings for a while, to change the scenery, the people, the atmosphere, the daily rhythm. To get away from it all, give up the chores and routine. To replace the peace and quiet of Werenhus with the buzz and chatter of the Station of Polish Academy of Sciences, packed with people in the summer. Such a 'weekend outing' in order to refresh your mind, the thing that turns out to be so useful in our urban civilisation in lower latitudes, seems to be our natural need even in this peaceful and pure world. The necessity for change and variety, even for a short moment, seems to be somehow inborn in human beings. Even when we are in a safe, nice and beautiful place which we like – and Werenhus was certainly such a place for us – nonetheless from time to time, we feel compelled to leave this place for a while and go to some other destination, even if it was just a couple of kilometres away.

The expedition to the base becomes a kind of private holiday for everyone who sets out on it. Even if they go there on urgent business. A holiday as opposed to 'everyday'. We need our own little holidays, celebrated privately, off the official calendar, on the fringes of national or religious celebrations, no matter what place we inhabit at a given moment. It is possible that some spots on Earth, such as the Arctic, for example, release in us the need to celebrate as well as appreciate moments and their significance. In what other way can you save yourself from the sea of monotony, where there is no difference between day and night – because the night has become the day and you can see daylight 24 hours non-stop. Celebrating is not just breaking off from the routine. It is also, and perhaps first of all, being with others. Experiencing a sense of togetherness. Sharing your time and space with other people. Irrespective of the country, culture or religion, a time of holiday is very often a time of moving about. The need to celebrate a holiday with those close to you – your family, friends or mates – puts crowds of people on the move. They simply want to be together.

Becoming a part of this intercultural and timeless trend, we set off towards the base on Saturday morning. Obviously we had our name-day presents with us which were inventive in varying degree. The more creative ones were cards for the 'name-day boys'. And they were no mean cards, made from usual paper, oh no! They were a solid piece of work. Literally, as they were made of one of the hardest rocks available in the Werenhus area, quartzite, which have extraordinary colouring. Apart from traditional white quartzites in this area, there are green ones as well, and, a real rarity, green and white quartzites in which both colours blend and melt creating fanciful patterns – lines, checks, smudges, shades and even circles. In addition to that, they break up into ideally flat 'slates', which makes them perfect for birthday or name-day cards. Initially, the best wishes were to be engraved on them, however, no man in our group was strong enough for this job. They all lost their battle with the hard quartzite. The only thing we could do was write inscriptions with a waterproof marker. As a final touch we stuck a dried tundra flower in the corner of each slate. The less inventive present was far less original – it was a bottle of yellowish liquid, a lemon cordial called 'Cytrynowka' in Polish (pronounced 'Tseetreenoovka') – made by fellow hydrologists who are experts and unrivalled in this art.

After a few hours of marching, we reached the base in the late afternoon. We could already see, from far away, quite a crowd hanging around between the building of the station and Banachowka ('Bhanahoovka') Boathouse. It was there, in the boathouse, that the celebration was taking place. It was an ideal spot for a real barbecue. We were lucky. One of the name-day boys was a cook. No wonder we could smell the enticing aromas of freshly prepared food, even more tempting after so many hours of tiresome marching. Christopher the Cook set himself an ambitious task, and carried it out to perfection. The finesse, sophistication and variety of the feast gained wide recognition, especially when you realised that all this fancy food was served in the immediate vicinity of the North Pole.

'You are here at last!' One of the Christophers noticed us from afar and came out to meet us: 'I'm so glad to see you. Thank you for coming.' He greeted us with a strong handshake.

This simple greeting was very powerful. We had known one another for a short time only. In normal conditions it would be far too short to make friends, too few conversations to create a real bond. However, in Spitsbergen conditions, everything gets accelerated and intensified, especially human relationships. They develop very quickly and intensely and may collapse in the same rapid and abrupt manner. It is enough sometimes to strike up a conversation with a stranger, and then to have a lifelong friend (or enemy) at least for the whole stay in Spitsbergen. An incredible intensity and concentration of various relations, bonds, ties and arrangements – building and breaking. It could generate faith in a person or destroy it. A world of all kinds of human emotions, intensified and confined to this little space in which we all dwelt, willingly, but it was actually a maze with no way out. You had no escape until the ship came into harbour to collect you. You could not avoid getting entangled in a complex network of human relationships.

But in Christopher's voice you could hear real joy. He was genuinely waiting for us and was happy to see us. I was happy too. Joy is found because you are meeting up and spending some time together.

'We've brought you something. Here you are, this is your name-day card. It may look small but you can't say it's light.'

'It's beautiful! And you've made it by yourselves? It's the first time in my life I've been given such a personal gift, and hand-made!' Christopher is moved, it looks like there are tears in his eyes. 'Thanks a lot. Cheers, guys!'

And it was just such a simple thing, one of these bits and bobs – a piece of rock, a small plant and that vulgar thick marker – but what else could you spontaneously conjure in crude field conditions? Sometimes you do not realise how powerful a seemingly worthless 'little something' can be. How meaningful it may become to another person. It turns out that even the smallest gesture or behaviour can rise to a completely different level. That is why you have to be extra careful not to hurt anyone, but on the other hand, you do not need much to make somebody happy. The second of the celebrating Christophers, who also received that stony name-day card, has said to me recently that he still has it at home. After so many years! It has been resting on the shelf displayed in a most visible place all this time. I did not expect him to add so much weight to a simple piece of rock. But it is not really the rock we are talking about now.

'That's not all, we've got something else, too. A bottle. With a precious liquid. Drink with due caution.' Laughing heartily we hand to Christopher the second part of our present.

'I can't promise you that. You must excuse the name-day boy. It will come in very handy today, nay indispensable,' this time there was a sparkle in his eye, 'Come, you must be very hungry and the party has already started at Banachowka Boathouse.' He led us into the midst of the celebrating crowd.

'The palms! I can't believe my eyes!' We have just noticed a cluster of palms 'growing' on the shore. They were made of paper, had brown trunks and impressive plumes of dark-green ragged leaves. 'Welcome to Hornsund Beach' read the banner beneath it.

'Tropics! Damn it, real tropics! I hadn't expected the global warming to happen so soon, did you?' Heniu looked as if he was very worried about the change of the environmental weather pattern. 'I should have packed my flowery Hawaiian shirt. I can't do without it tonight.'

We mingled with the crowd. We shook hands with our friends from the base, enjoyed conversations, took photos under the palms (not that our fleece jackets and anoraks matched the tropical atmosphere of the place), watched a swimming competition. Yes, that's right. Some cold-water enthusiasts decided to go into the ice-cold sea to swim (a couple of metres) in the so-called 'Walruses' Races'. There was even dancing. If you think that it is impossible to do rock-and-roll moves in wellington boots, you are very much mistaken. It is possible even when a thick layer of stones rolls under your feet and you get 'bogged' down in pebbles. Dancing and talking went on until late in the night. Some conversations turned into less serious discussions, some into more serious disputes. Everybody was overwhelmed by a serene and carefree atmosphere. It was Saturday night, after all. We spent it in a traditional way, resting and forgetting about everyday problems. We owed it to ourselves after the whole week of intense work. In the Arctic world where the distinction of days of the week seems to make no sense, we wanted to stick to it. We needed the same balance, which we were used to in a different reality. The time for work and the time for rest. The time for being together.

The next morning we woke to an alarm.

'A bear! A polar bear at Banachowka Boathouse!'

Indeed, there was a bear. We could see its massive white figure from the windows of the base. He was standing on his rear paws, which made him look even bigger, and was banging on the big metal door of the boathouse.

'Look at this "teddy bear". He was probably lured out by the scent of yesterday's feast. He's a bit late for the barbecue, isn't he?' We could joke at will as we were a safe distance away.

Maybe he was indeed lured by the feast, maybe he came out of curiosity. Being a lone wolf, or rather 'a lone bear', he was puzzled by our 'herd' or 'pack' – our group and the energy that comes from being together. Yesterday's holiday and the joy of celebration must have left some undefined scent in the air, imperceptible to our insensitive nostrils. Perhaps it was what fascinated him? He came to find out why these funny beings, tiny lanky figures, which use only their rear legs for walking, come together and insist on staying in flocks. A phenomenon most incomprehensible for an Arctic loner.

Daily contact with other people was not expressed in such a spectacular way as on special occasions, like birthdays or name days. Most often it was just visiting the neighbours. Of all Polish research stations in the Arctic, the researchers based at Hornsund are privileged being situated within walking distances. 'Within arm's reach' from Werenhus, that is, within half an hour's march, there was an old trapper's hut, Hyttevika. In the summer it was usually taken over by the researchers from the Cracow AGH University of Science and Technology. We were joking that these two huts, ours and theirs, made up our 'village', as opposed to a more distant and more civilised 'city', that is the Station of Polish Academy of Sciences.

When one of the teams was doing field work in the neighbourhood or coming back from a longer expedition, there was a custom of dropping in for tea, or something stronger, to warm up. Sometimes lunch would be available if you were lucky to arrive at just the right time. Sometimes these were planned visits, when you came round just to talk to others. From time to time, you felt an urge to leave the circle of people you *have to* live with, in one small space, and go to those you *want to* stay with, in an equally small but *different* space. It is a most natural need to reach out, abandon your confinement, leave for a while the people and places too familiar to you.

❁   ❁   ❁

The feeling of being a part of a community is very strong in Spitsbergen. However, it may have different facets. On the one hand, big parties, far-away visits to the base or short visits to your neighbours. On the other hand, a more subtle feeling of the bond with others can be experienced when, for instance, you are waiting for someone to come back from a long route after a day's work, or you come back 'home', to Werenhus, from the base.

'Werenhus, Werenhus, base calls you. Over.' I tried to make contact with the boys in Werenhus. Theoretically, there should be someone in the hut. I was right.

'This is Werenhus, hello Aga ('Ahgha'), when are you coming back?'

'That's the reason I'm calling. I'm coming today. Jurek ('Yurek') has decided to come along. He has some business for you, too. We're going to set off in an hour, so I think we'll reach you late. Don't wait for us, just go to bed. We can't say exactly what time we'll be there.'

'OK, no problem. We'll be sitting around anyway. The others are still out in the field. There will be some time before they are back. You know how it is.'

'Right, see you later then.'

'It will be good to see you again. You've been missed here. We definitely need a lady here to teach us some manners. The female presence always "soothes the savage beast".'

'Yes, surely there is no one to cook and clean for you,' I replied with a sneer.

However, my sneering was utterly unjust. In the Arctic conditions, and definitely in Werenhus, there was full equality. Everybody shared the same cleaning or cooking duties. Nobody protested. Everyone thought it was most natural, the joint responsibility within our common house and vital in the efficient running of the household. I felt suddenly I had gone too far with my comment.

'Just joking,' I added quickly, 'I am also happy to go back home. I miss the peace and quiet of Werenhus…'

'OK, see you then. Mind your step and watch out for the bears on your way.'

'We'll try, goodbye. Over and out.'

Reporting before setting out on a longer trip is obligatory due to safety reasons. There is a special 'in-and-out' book in the base. Each person going out is obliged to enter their name into it, write where they are going, when they plan to come back and the time for raising the emergency alarm and starting the search. Fortunately, there hasn't been an alarm for a long time. Before your departure you send a radio message to the base or Werenhus and report again on your arrival. This is also a kind of responsibility, not only for yourself, but also for others. You can't be careless. You mustn't forget about your return report. Somebody is waiting for your message and may be at their wits' end if there isn't one. You already know you've safely reached your destination, but others don't. Responsibility works both ways.

The journey from the base lasted forever in spite of good weather. The day was nice and windless, but the heavy backpack was chafing my shoulders, and my wellies sank deep into soft moss growing on peat. We needed to stop frequently. It was well after one o'clock in the morning when we finally saw the roof of Werenhus. 'They must be all asleep now,' I thought regretfully, because I had hoped we would reach the hut earlier. We crossed the footbridge over the home river and began to take off our rucksacks and anoraks outside before going into the house. We didn't want to make any noise in the hallway and wake up the sleeping. And then, suddenly, the door opened with a bang and the whole group of 'sleepyheads' poured out into the yard singing a 'welcome song' to us.

'Welcome to our humble abode at Werenhus! And as the old Polish custom has it, help yourselves to our modest piece of bread and a pinch of salt. And of course something else to build up your strength after a long journey.' Mirek ('Meerek') and Heniu emerged from the hut, solemnly carrying a tray with pumpernickel bread, a small salt shaker and a glass of vodka. Pumpernickel is pressed wholemeal bread, which keeps fresh and is edible even after several years spent in the Werenhus larder, in the vacuum packaging of course. Far beyond its 'Best before', it's just 'Best after'. The boys gave me such a warm welcome as if I had been away from home for a year and not for a couple of days. My darlings! Only they could think up something like that.

'You are crazy! Didn't I tell you to go to sleep. You shouldn't have stayed up!' I sounded indignant but in fact I was so happy they had waited.

It is so important to have a place where somebody is waiting for you, where you can come back with joy because they will receive you with open arms and hearts. Even if there is no bread or salt for a traditional Polish welcome.

❀   ❀   ❀

We need closeness with others but sometimes what we need even more is solitude. Contrary to appearances, it is not easily found in the apparently desolate Arctic.

'Werenhus, Werenhus, base speaking. You will have visitors on Saturday. A few people from the base. If the weather stays clear, we'll come in dinghies. There'll be around five or six of us. We'd love to stay overnight for Sunday. Is that OK?'

'Sure, you are very welcome. There is plenty of room, no problem with accommodation.'

What other words could you possibly say? Even if you knew that 14 square metres of the hut provided no luxury, especially if it had to hold a dozen of people. In fact, there is no other reply in the Arctic, where the doors of all huts are open to everybody. The only problem is that it has been several Sundays in a row that we have had visitors. And even during the week. More and more pleasure boats and research boats come to Hornsund, more and more people want to go on longer outings. Werenhus serves this purpose perfectly well. In the last few days we have entertained a couple of Americans, two Dutch women, one German, not to mention the crowd of our fellow countrymen, who have dropped in to pay us a visit since the beginning of the summer season. It is so nice to be able to accommodate fatigued wanderers in a cosy hut and strengthen them with hot tea and nutritious soup. But why do they come in dozens? Why do they crowd in? Why can't we just do our work or enjoy the peace and quiet of our 'own' home? It makes you feel rebellious inside. You revolt against never-ending hullabaloo and trivial small talk. Your mind demands peace and your body some empty space. The fact that so many people, and very often strangers, are living in such cramped conditions makes you feel like running away. And every day the feeling gets stronger and stronger. You get nervous and annoyed even by close friends or people you know well, if you are forced to stay in their presence constantly. But at Werenhus there is no nook where you can hide and protect yourself from the rising cacophony and continuous movement of bodies, bumping into each other, being in the way, within this cramped and narrow space we all inhabit. Even our hut begins to protest against the 'population density' inside it. The wooden ceiling, being at the same time the upper floor, starts to bend down dangerously under the weight of too many people sleeping upstairs. The door from the kitchen to the small laboratory room, where more people are sleeping, won't close. It is blocked by the lowered ceiling. The house sends its warning signals. It is too heavy a burden for it to bear. With its bent-down upper floor, the house makes a wry face, disgruntled at the noise and excessive exploitation of its tiny area. It is only when the last visitors go over the footbridge, and disappear behind the rocks protruding against the skyline, that the wooden walls of the house relax and start to breathe freely, enjoying their regained freedom.

The Arctic experiment is going on. Every year, new crowds of people set off on a journey into the icy desert. What are they looking for? Solitude? Or maybe just the opposite – togetherness or community? The need for bonds and belonging is constantly mixed with the need for isolation, independence and solitary contemplation of the world. Will the Arctic intensity of these two opposites teach us how to keep the balance between them? After all, it is just this balance, the mental equilibrium, we are all straining to find.

7 Past

We were wandering about with our eyes fixed on the ground,
overwhelmed by the same archaeologists' emotion which is none other than
being touched by the feeling of human solidarity in time.

Jan Jozef Szczepanski, *The Polar Bear Bay*

There were just a couple of days left to our departure. All our field work was finished for that season so we could afford to wander around casually. We finally had time to relish the scenery. However, on that day the weather did not entice anybody to do any walking at all. Werenhus and its vicinity were enveloped in a thick milky fog. It was tangible. It effectively narrowed the horizon to the circle of a few metres. In spite of that, someone suggested going out.

'Come on, couch potatoes. Let's go walkies. How long can you linger within four walls? Don't you need some fresh air?'

Yes, we did need some fresh air. So in no time a group of walking enthusiasts was ready to set off.

'Where shall we go then? We haven't decided on a route or direction yet.'

'We can't go mountain climbing in this weather,' we all agreed on that one. The choice was limited. The coastline, to the right or to the left.

'To be honest, I'm fed up with the route towards the base. All my field research was in that section and I know every inch of ground there.'

'Right, it's dead boring in that direction.'

'So the choice is simple, there is only Elveflya left.'

Fierce icy-cold rivers on the surface of the Werenskiold Glacier.

Elveflya is a vast coastal plain. It starts just behind our shelter and extends northwards, in the opposite direction to our frequent route towards the south east, towards the Station of Polish Academy of Sciences. It is enough to cross a white water called the Glacier River behind the house to notice that the uneven ground of rock-and-peat tundra has been replaced by the flat and smooth surface of compacted gravel pebbles. This flat surface, so different from the undulating land south of Werenhus, came into being thanks to a river that used to flow in this area. Originating from the local glacier Werenskiold, the river would take innumerable rocks and stones from its massive bulk and then drop them at its mouth by the sea. With the passage of time the volume of sediment brought by the river had grown to a colossal size – the size of today's Elveflya. And then, one day, the river changed its course. It created a new channel and bypassed its old river bed. The material carried in the water started to be deposited elsewhere. Elveflya became silent and motionless. Its development ceased when the river abandoned its territory and could not build further without

Countless channels and streams – the braided river on Elveflya.

the load brought by the flowing river. It could only remain statically or shrink under the impact of storm waves.

In the milky white glow of the fog, the surface of Elveflya appeared to be even more deadly and still than ever. The Earth seemed to have lost all its form. The tangible hardness of gravel merged with the elusive softness of misty air, as if there was no physical difference between them. Only, once in a while, blurred contours of dark grey shadows emerged from the thick coat of the fog, single rocks coming up towards the sky from a monotonous flat ground. They were once islands. When their silhouettes began to show faintly in the mist we had to stop and fix our eyes on them, just in case a darker fragment of the landscape should move. It might have been a bear! When such a fog envelopes the world it is impossible to distinguish rocks from animals. It is only the movement, the merest twitch, that can give them away and help you realise what you see is 'real life' rather than 'still life'. That time we were lucky, no shape budged.

We followed the coastline. It was the safest solution. We were making for a small group of rocks in the vicinity of Cape Kvislodden, in the central coastal part of Elveflya. None of us had ever been there before. That place had never been 'en route'. Our way there reminded me of an obstacle course, a hurdle race. Instead of clearing hurdles we 'cleared' logs, as the whole shore was strewn with driftwood. Whitened by the sea salt, stripped of their bark, the logs were lying disorderly on the beach like matches or giant's jackstraws. In the woodless Arctic, driftwood is very precious. It is collected to be used as firewood. However, in that remote place, far away from human dwellings, nobody needed it. The logs could stay where they were stranded, left alone at perhaps the last stage of their long journey. Most of them were seafarers, 'runaways' from Siberia, floating first down the northbound rivers or were victims

The 'escapers' from Siberian taiga.

of floods caused by the swollen rivers of northern Russia. Some timber bore traces of tools. It might have come from some vessel, ship or boat. Dead logs reminded me suddenly of bones scattered on a battlefield. The same white colour, the same chaotic layout, the same non-resemblance to their former shape of existence. Ugh, it gave me the creeps! The fog was fooling about with my imagination.

The contours of the rocks we were heading for came into view in front of us. With every step we took, they became more real and tangible.

'Look! There is a flagpole or mast over there.'

'Indeed, and quite tall.'

We were just approaching it. A dark vertical line of some unidentified standing object stood out against the light background of the mist.

'And I thought we were going to discover a completely virgin unexplored place.' sighed one of us.

Of course, we all knew that was impossible. At least not in this part of Spitsbergen, which had been described in detail and measured by a hundred-strong crowd of subsequent generations of scientists. After all, we were holding an exact topographical map of the shore we were treading on. But the air of mystery brought about by a misty veil enriched our fantasy. Is there any explorer in the world that does not dream of reaching a place where they will be the first human being ever touching it? To find your own, even the smallest, patch of ground that has not been discovered or touched by anybody else. A part of the world that could be only yours. Unfortunately, the tall wooden pole brought us back down to Earth, reminding us of the fact that the place we thought was ours had already been taken. There was no doubt that the pole had been erected by a human hand. Well, being an explorer nowadays is no easy task at all … but we still felt the passion of exploration burning inside. We did not know yet what kind of a place it was, what sort of a pole, who had put it there and what purpose it served.

We climbed up, not too high, onto a flat and wide rock. The thin wooden mast was fixed onto it. We also found some planks hammered into some kind of a cross or trestle fastened vertically onto the ground.

'What is this? A tomb?'

'Buried treasure?'

'Yes, pirates for sure…'

We carelessly got carried away by our imagination again. The real, sensible world did not exist any longer, it had been swallowed up by the fog. What the heck! Why should we hang onto rationalism so tightly? We started to make up incredible stories, until the voice of reason had the floor, ruining all our fun.

'I know what it is! These must be remains of a geodetic survey stand.' The voice was triumphant and we returned immediately from our fantasy world. Yes, each of us either heard or read about the first Polish scientific expeditions in this area of Spitsbergen.

What makes up the basis of all nature research is the description of the existing variety of phenomena and processes in a certain space. However, the researchers must first prepare such a space. The first explorers could not mark anything on the maps because these did not exist. Everything had to be created from scratch. In that age, the researchers did not have the complex measuring equipment, computers, lasers and satellites of today. Traditional methods did not fail – a network of geodetic survey marks and triangles, detailed topographic and triangular measurements, and the application of a stereo-grammetry method resulted in precise topographic maps of the whole area. It was painstaking, systematic and time-consuming work done by the whole team of pioneers who paved the way before us, the future explorers, who came a bit too late to find anything new. We were doomed to discover only the traces of the past. We were standing at such a geodetic standpoint. The wooden pole turned out to be a counterpart of a familiar triangular tower, while the trestles fixed onto the ground were remains of the structure designed for precise survey and calculation. It must have been the place where a theodolite was mounted.

We did not discover anything special. Nevertheless, we were overwhelmed by the explorers' passion. We were in one of the places where the history of scientific exploration of this part of the Arctic was born. If it hadn't been for the effort and work of those people unknown to us, who decades ago had been standing on the same spot, we wouldn't be here now. Even more traces of Arctic history, the history we now continue, can be found in articles, books and map sheets dispersed in libraries and collections all over the world. The traces that remained in the field do not stand out from the background so much – just a couple of wooden stakes, a few boards, apparently nothing much. As if they wanted to stay hidden, recognisable only by the initiated. But the fog was working in our favour, helping our imagination.

Suddenly the planks turn into a workstation. People are bending over sheets of paper, marking subsequent readings of measurements. They have difficulty withstanding strong winds blowing from the sea. There is no protection against the wind in this open area. But the job has to be completed as soon as possible. Others are waiting for it. You cannot tame a wild territory without giving it a shape, form and dimension. First things first! A map must be created. And so the measurements are being taken, subsequent columns of figures are being registered and then turned into the soft contour lines of a map.

It's time we went back. We were climbing down the rock. Having walked a few steps away, I turned around. I could hardly make out the thin shape of the wooden pole. But it was still there like a message from the past. To make us remember. To rescue the memory of those before us from oblivion. After all, it is the same history. Our history. The discovery of meagre remains of the former survey standpoint affected our frame of mind. We were all in a lofty mood. Was that also of the mist's making? It was still veiling the horizon. We were walking in silence.

'You know, a thought has just crossed my mind. Actually, the whole Arctic is like a giant museum of the past – distant and close, both of people and nature.'

There is utter silence. Nobody keeps up the conversation. Clearly, we all feel the same and ponder on it. Now we perceive the driftwood in a different way. It is also a sign of the past. It is a complete coincidence that it was found in this particular place. We hear Elveflya's gravel scrape beneath our feet. Elveflya itself is preserved in time, a remnant of the past, at least for the time being. The remnant of the world that used to exist before the river changed its course. The now-dead gravel river bed was once filled with a joyful murmur of the water streaming towards the sea. You can't resist the impression that the Arctic has been able to conserve history and let objects, places and forms persist in spite of their time having passed. They belong to different epochs and yet they lived on, creating a mosaic composed of shreds and crumbs of various worlds and ages.

Even more traces of the past from different epochs can be discovered in the puzzle of the Arctic landscape. More or less halfway between the base and Werenhus there is a huge whale bone, several metres long, lying on the shore. It is not snow-white any longer. It has become greyish and grown green in some spots due to a colony of algae. On both ends it has deep cuts or notches. One more trace of frozen history. This time the history of hunting. In the old days people used to hunt everything that moved both on the land and in the sea. The whale hunting in the Arctic seas reached its peak in the 17th century. In a short time most of the whales from this area were destroyed. However, people did not give up hunting these powerful sea mammals.

Sometimes beluga whales swim into Hornsund. These are white whales that were highly valued by ancient hunters. I saw them once. Five smooth, white and yellowish backs were rhythmically going over and under the waters of the fjord. It is said that catching a glimpse of them brings you good luck.

The whale bones that were worked on the shore and then abandoned now belong to Norwegian national heritage, according to the law of Norway. Would that be some kind of belated compensation and meagre indemnification for previous cruelty to living creatures? Norwegian law protects everything that is found on the seashore, namely, the material remains of animals, buildings, everyday articles both of archaeological value and of quite recent origin. Objects bearing witness both to great achievements and disgraceful acts. All of them are treated with equal respect and by order of the law must be left where they were found. After all, they are traces of national history. No matter how good or bad, whether generating pride or shame, they are nevertheless ours: the history that shapes our unique identity and character. Who would we be without our history? Without these tiny events that weave the cloth of our life? Even if we wanted to forget about some of them, delete them from our memory, we would not be able to run away from them. They are stuck in us like the notches in whale bones. The bones that are intrinsic to the Arctic coast, even if they are the sign of disreputable acts of the human race. But we cannot deny the fact of who we are and what has shaped us. This Norwegian law is wisely conceived, since we cannot renounce our roots, it might be better to protect our past, appreciate and value it. Maybe it is the way to come to terms with it.

Apart from the whale bones, there are numerous remains of old traps for foxes and bears set by trappers. If you are not familiar with the hunting chronicles of Spitsbergen, you will probably not recognise that piled up stones, fragments of broken planks or square grids made of wooden bars are remains of tricky devices – cage traps or ratchet traps that facilitated the trappers' job greatly. The most sophisticated ones were constructed as automatic shooting traps. An animal was lured inside by the scent of the bait, and while it was pulling it and struggling inside triggered thus a specially mounted gun with a shortened barrel. The trapper's task was to follow the usual route, from trap to trap, and collect his take. Very often during our walks in tundra we came across such remains, reminding us of the disgraceful past.

Unfortunately, the researchers also left a lot of mess behind. Especially in the neighbourhood of the base you can trip over all sorts of things, like metal bars, partly hidden in the ground, wires and pipes of some mysterious application. A long time ago someone made a good use of them, but are they still serving their purpose? Who can guess now what they were actually used for? Can they ever become useful again in the future? And maybe these metal, rusty and distorted objects will be the only items that we will leave behind? A huge scrap yard. I wonder if future generations of Norwegians will want to protect it as a part of their historical heritage?

I definitely prefer ancient history, primeval history. It seems that the traces left by primitive people were pure and innocent. Like the remains of the huts of the first inhabitants in Spitsbergen, the Pomors who started coming from the territory of northern Russia in the 15th and 16th centuries and settled in small hunting settlements on Arctic islands.

I don't remember exactly who, or when, showed us the remains of these settlements. I don't think I would be able to find them again on my own. But they are still there, somewhere on the coast, between the base and Werenhus. Like everything else – this area housed our whole Arctic world. Walking at a brisk pace I would definitely have gone past them, not noticing evenly laid stones and wooden beams covered by a thick layer of moss, making them barely visible against the tundra. If you looked hard, you could see an outline of a rhomboid shape. So that was the site where the first dwellers of this inhospitable land lived. One more piece of an Arctic jigsaw puzzle of different times and histories.

We can go back even further into the past, reach the very beginnings of history, long before we humans arrived. There are few places in the world such as the Arctic that open a window on the Earth's secrets in such a clear and distinctive way. Bare rock walls reveal subsequent rock layers and levels. We can follow their history, make guesses about the circumstances of their development, admire fossils from the time when you could enjoy warm seas and luxuriant forests in the Arctic. You feel the peace embodied in the horizontal layers of undisturbed sediments. But also you recognise moments of the turbulent and stormy past, when massive forces from within the Earth's crust crushed and pressed, stretched and rolled the rocks, as if they were plasticine. This time of unrest was recorded forever in the clearly visible curves and bends of folded rock layers, abruptly broken by fault lines. Even the most remote past is still legible in powerful rock structures. The moments of peace and quiet as well as shocks and disasters in our human life are not recorded as deeply as in the rock. They pass, go by, leaving ephemeral traces in our psyche. Unless someone, at a moment of great pain, composes some music or writes a poem. These could be our human counterparts of rock faults or folds. Permanent remains, traces of important events when a new structure is created – a man or a rock.

I traverse the shore. The gravel beach full of colourful pebbles crunches under my boots. I bend down and pick up a couple of round stones. Each one has its own past recorded within it. I discern the traces of huge structures of rock walls reflected in these tiny crumbs. A tangle of veins, intersections of multicoloured layers, spots, holes, cracks or scratches, and even miniature folds and faults. Each stone bears its own individual history. At the same time it is also a part of some wider common history, a history of millions of years of geological past. Doesn't it remind us of something? Of some particularly coincident analogy? Individuality inscribed within community. Originality and uniqueness paradoxically embedded in the constant cycle of the ages. The traces of the past surround us everywhere. They are even inside us.

I close my hand. I put the colourful pebbles into my pocket. They will find their place on the shelf at my home. After my return. That is – in the future.

8 Hus

(…) It has always seemed to me that this tranquillity facing extinction
was something worth saving, something essential, like a ballast on the ship,
keeping all human communities in balance.
What other thing could you possibly oppose to an increasing rush?

Jan Jozef Szczepanski, *The Polar Bear Bay*

A thin streak of light crept along an old floorboard in Hyttevika, a former trap-pers' hut on the northern coast of Hornsund. A ray of sunshine in the middle of the dark bowels of the hus. Why did we not notice that ray before? After a few minutes of 'investigation' and struggling through junk in our stock room, we knew.

'You see over there?' Szymon ('Sheemon') pointed at the hus wall. 'There is a small hole in the wooden plank. A knot may have fallen out or it could have been a former firing port. You know, one of those holes the trappers would cut out in the hus walls to make hunting easier.'

'How is it possible that we haven't seen it before? We've been already living here for a couple of days.' I tried to find a logical explanation for a sudden appearance of the patch of sunlight.

'Yeah, but we haven't been so careless yet to leave the door to the cold hallway and stock room wide open. We were careful not to chill the room that took so much effort to warm up,' Szymon's practical mind could not think of anything else.

We moved a huge chest with our food supplies out of the way. We did the same with a few old planks kept in the stock room, nobody knows what for. Now we could

63

easily peep out of our newly discovered 'window'. Just with one eye, but we could see quite a way away: a bit of the coastline and shore rocks in the background and in the foreground our intensely green moss 'lawn' in front of the hut. Quite an impressive panorama for a window only a couple of centimetres in diameter.

Some may be surprised at our reaction. Nothing important happened. A knot fell out of the board or somebody cut out a piece of wood. No big deal. A ray of sunshine got into the hut – that's normal too. No reason for such delight. Yes, that is all true. However, when you are living in the hus, far away from any civilisation, at the northern edge of the world, surrounded only by the sea, mountains and glaciers, then even the most trivial everyday activity may become a miracle, discovery or reason for joy. And no joy is banal. At the same time, it is a shame that in our ordinary everyday lives we do not notice how much joy is hidden in simple things because we always seem to be in such a hurry. We do not perceive the fact that we can enjoy even an ephemeral beam of light appearing on the dark floor. First we must notice it.

We came back to the warm 'living room'. The light beam was still there decorating the floor. In the sunlight we could clearly see how uneven the ancient floor made of tatty planks was. We had paid no attention to that shabby surface before. It was only then that we started to take in the fact that there was something more beneath our feet. We tried to read the history written in its cracks and scratches. There was a gap between the boards. It might have been widened by the ice freezing in the slit. After all, the changing of the floor into an 'ice rink' is common in the Arctic winter. A small but visible dent in one of the planks – maybe a mark left by some heavy object that fell down. The floor around the stove was much darker, blackened and bearing traces of soot. It was proof that all dwellers of the hut were persistently driving off the winter, warding it off with fire. There were many cuts and scars we could not decipher. The old floor preserved the memory of the old days, past events, former inhabitants. In the same way the wrinkles on your face preserve the traces of your own individual victories and defeats.

Hyttevika is a venerable old hut. It was built in the early twentieth century and has just celebrated its 100-year anniversary. The hus walls must have seen a thing or two during its life, big and small dramas, dilemmas, joys and successes. First, of the trappers who used to live there. The trappers who were waiting patiently for their game, planning carefully the network of their traps and snares. Their era is gone now. In 1973 a national park was established in this area of Spitsbergen and all hunting was forbidden. The majority of trappers' huts began to serve new inhabitants – the crowds of researchers who were pouring into the Arctic regions. The interiors of the huts, which used to smell of fresh game and tanned skins of Arctic foxes, bears and seals, were filled now with piles of books, notes, maps, measuring equipment and

Reindeer almost in the 'house garden'.

quite recently with cutting-edge technology, such as laptops, palmtops, GPSs and satellite phones. A modern version of hunting – not for animals, but for a scientific discovery or breakthrough.

The hus walls remember the hunters' happiness with their abundant take and successful hunting season, which allowed them not to worry about their survival. But within these walls there is also pain and rage of failure and the spectre of famine in the winter when the season was not satisfactory and there were too few pelts for sale. The hus beams preserve the joy of the researchers who successfully completed the season and were happy with performed measurements as well as collected samples and exhibits. But there is also sadness and disappointment when the research did not go well or the theories they strongly believed in proved erroneous.

Trappers' and researchers' successes and failures are not the only emotions built into these old overstrained walls of the hus. They include a much wider palette of casual feelings and activities:

'What shall we have for dinner today?'

'Any volunteers to make the fire? As usual, none. You're not too keen on that job.'

'Just look at the fantastic shapes of the ice blocks in the bay! They have only come this morning.'

'Oh, no! It's raining again. Does it ever stop here? We won't be on time with our field project…'

'Jasiu ('Yashiu') and Bartek ('Bhartek') haven't come back yet. They've been out for nine hours. They should be back by now. I'm starting to worry.'

'I'm putting the kettle on, anyone fancy some tea?'

For decades the hus has been filled with thousands of various, more or less important, matters that engage the human mind. Survival, work and leisure, solitude and cooperation. Conflicts you cannot avoid while living in such a tiny space along with a group of individuals. But also the utmost confidence and trust you have in somebody close to you with whom you share your dwelling. For over 100 years the hus walls echoed with some bad words or curses uttered in outrage or fury. But they also witnessed soft whispers of affection and trusting love. Even a baby was born here many years ago, in the trappers' time. It is just several square metres of wooden floor and low walls, but inside you have a whole new world, changing from year to year, from season to season, each time with the coming and going of its occupants. It is these stories from a close or distant past, fascinating or dull, that the hus wants to tell us with its creaking floor, with every beam in the wall, the permeating smell of smoke, wood burning in the stove and with every single item collected there. It is amazing that a tiny hut built somewhere at the end of the world can encompass such a number of artefacts.

We will never understand these stories fully. We will never meet the person whose hands hung a checked curtain in the hus window, constructed the wooden bunk bed, table and bench; the hands that put a big collection of Norwegian books onto the shelves, which look quite dog-eared now; the hands that hammered nails into the walls, serving now as hangers; the hands that did a lot of other small jobs to make the hus become a home. Our home now. After this house, which was built over a century ago, the whole bay got its name. Hyttevika – means no other thing than the Bay of the House or the Bay of the Hut – Home Bay. The very building has the same name because it really is a home bay for us, a warm and safe haven. During the first expeditions, however, the explorers used a far less romantic and affectionate name for this place. They used to call it the 'sub-base'.

We sense the past around us. It comes up again and again in small items found in the hut. But the past is beyond us. And that's the way it is. Now it is time for us to create our history of friendship with the hut. Now our feet tread on the wooden boards, leaving our traces. Maybe someone will notice them, some day in the future, in a ray of sunshine that will throw light on the hus interior and its mysteries. We are immersed in the extraordinary atmosphere of Hyttevika, which is full of the past. It surrounds us like the scent of smoke from the stove in our hair, skin and clothes. We are beginning to write a new chapter in the hut's rich history. We have our share in it, which is not going to be recognised in the years to come and no one will attribute it to us. A new string and wood structure for drying clothes over the stove, a stone candlestick made from pebbles found on the shore, a renewed inscription, 'Hyttevika', above the entrance door, which was burnt into wood with a hot nail by Szymon. Brief moments recorded in small objects, remembrance of the time when we could call hus our home. A short interval – between those whose time in Hyttevika is over and those who will come after us.

The hus has been patiently collecting all stories and items. It is astonishing how many extraordinary treasures you can ferret out by searching every nook and cranny. There are countless cubby-holes and hiding places there. The huts had to be most functional as they provided accommodation for trappers for at least half a year in this inhospitable environment. For decades, people have brought many items that would secure them against danger or let them live in a self-sufficient way. With each subsequent season the number has grown. In our leisure time after work or during rainy days we go treasure hunting. Our discoveries are always surprising. We are astonished at the human resourcefulness that brought to this remote place almost anything you can think of. We find a stock of rusty nails that were forgotten a long time ago, two packets of old candles (why on earth did they send for the new ones now?), glass saucers and decanters, coasters cut out of some plastic whose purpose remains more or less mysterious, a worn-out sleeping bag, a set of strings and ropes, a small box of safety pins and drawing pins, bandages yellowed with age and many other finds. With a bit of imagination and inventiveness you can build or construct almost everything that could be needed. There are stocks of food too. Some articles were left by the previous expeditions, and new teams always bring fresh supplies. It would be impossible to die of starvation here unless you are very particular about the expiry date. It turns out that bread in vacuum packages, tinned food or powdered soups, which are several years old, taste delicious, especially after a whole day of work in the wind or drizzle. Not to mention custard or jelly delicacies. Who would ever think of throwing them away, even if their sell-by date is three or four years past? It is strange that so many objects can be found in such a small space. Even stranger, you do not have the impression that the place is cramped. Oh no! Most of the 'treasures' are hidden out of sight, popping up now and then when a discovery is made.

The interior of the hut looks austere and severe as befits a decent Scandinavian house. It must be neat and functional. There is a wide bunk bed in the corner, a wooden bench along the wall, a bookshelf above it. At the other side of the room there is a small cast-iron stove with an intricate grating on the glass doors, just behind it a huge pile of wood cut into pieces. Next to it, you can see a cupboard equipped with a full set of pots and pans, mugs and plates – of different sizes, colours and origin. All of them rather the worse for wear but that does not matter much. There is also a table in front of the cupboard and two chairs, although they could be considered armchairs, being covered by soft animal skins. This is our living room. You go out of it into a hallway that serves different purposes depending on the demand. At one time it is a kitchen where we set up our cooking facilities, namely portable gas cookers. Then it turns into a bathroom where we place a bowl of hot water, which has been warmed up on the stove. From the hallway you enter another room. It is used as a depot now, but it can also serve as a bedroom if there are more people around. That's the whole hut, covered with tar paper on the roof. It is perched low, close to the rocky ground, as if its builders wanted it to put down roots. You can barely see it at a distance. Its dark silhouette blurs with the background, with surrounding rocks as well as the brown green and reddish colours of tundra.

In the vastness of the Arctic this inconspicuous building is our home and safe haven. This fact is difficult to comprehend when you are looking at this tiny little thing squeezed between the sea and the rocky slope of the Gullichsenfjellet mountain range. The hut was built on the strip of land in its narrowest section between the water and land. Polar bears going from the west to the east in their annual wandering had no other way but to walk in front of the hunter's windows. The bears always went down a treat with hunters. They were a real bargain. In Norwegian the Hornsund shores are called 'Isbjørnpromenade', which means the Promenade of Polar Bears. Well, even today we take the consequences of this location being on the way and in the way of bears' wanderings. But now we are definitely less keen to meet the white king of the Arctic eye to eye.

⊛ ⊛ ⊛

Hyttevika is situated not only on the route of polar bears' wanderings but also on the way of polar explorers' excursions. The location between the Station of Polish Academy of Sciences and Werenhus makes it a comfortable stopover in a walk of a dozen or so kilometres. All the people walking along this simplest coastline 'road' drop in at Hyttevika hut. So one morning we were going to have guests. A few friends had called us on the radio and announced their visit the next day on their way back from Werenhus to the base. The guests were coming for tea. It is wonderful, meeting the people you know and like. Especially as for a couple of days we have not seen

A horse shoe at the entrance to Hyttevika – good luck for all the inhabitants and guests.

any living creatures apart from Arctic foxes, reindeer and innumerable birds. Except for brief messages sent through our shortwave radio, we were completely cut off from civilisation. It will be so nice to see familiar faces again and listen to the latest news and gossip from the wider world of Werenhus and the base. The instincts of the hostess stirred inside me. After all I had been the Lady of Hyttevika for over a week. I wanted to do my best and entertain our first guests in the best possible way, and there is nothing more important for the homemaker to hear than that the guests are feeling welcome in their house. I was happy that I could have some visitors. I wanted to look after those weary wanderers, to make them feel safe and comfy. Even ordinary tea has an extraordinary power when drunk together with others at the table. It signifies friendship between those who come and those who welcome them. The far North teaches us to appreciate the significance of open doors – leading to the cosy home with hot tea waiting on the table. It isn't much but it means a great deal. That is the reason I was so eager to play my role as a hus homemaker well.

On the very day of the expected visit I was woken up by loud shuffling on the gravel beach outside. I looked dazedly at my watch. It made my blood run cold.

Mother reindeer concerned that her youngster is following.

70

It's so early! And the guests have already arrived. We aren't ready yet!

The shuffling became even clearer. 'Well, let's face it, if I don't get up immediately I will have to open the doors wearing my pyjamas.' I got dressed in a jiffy, not wanting to welcome the visitors in this unbecoming way. The shuffling approached and sounded just outside the hus walls. As befits the hostess, I decided to go out and meet my guests on the doorstep. I struggled for a while with the sophisticated mechanism of the lock barring the door primarily against the bears. I poked my nose outside and was just about to walk out with a welcoming greeting when I saw our 'visitors'. Next to the hut, a couple of metres away from the entrance, there was a large polar bear. He was lying casually beside big rubbish bags and was fishing out all things potentially edible. The bags were supposed to have been taken by the Norwegians who had been renovating Hyttevika hut, but they hadn't done it yet. The bags' contents were scattered all over the beach, and the bear was cleaning it up. He was so absorbed in his activity that he took no notice of the noise made by the door. He enthusiastically kept on digging out treasures from the bag with his right paw while holding the sack with his left paw. If I was a trapper in the old days, I would definitely be delighted at such an opportunity. It would have been an easy catch, so the trappers would have probably got very excited about it. But I was not one of them. I slammed the door immediately, barred it inside, quickly and skilfully as never before.

'Szymon! There is a bear outside!' I rushed into the living room. I thanked God I was not alone to welcome such a 'guest', who in the meantime made himself comfortable in front of the entrance.

We came out of the hut after a few minutes, this time armed with pots and ladles. We were banging against them with all our strength. Such percussion, making that horrible clatter, was just unbearable. After a while we were totally deafened. And the bear? During the whole 'concert' performed by us with such zeal he raised his head only once and looked in our direction. Hmm, did it only appear to me, or did I really see a pitiful look in his eye? He was completely ignoring our presence as well as the infernal noise we were making. He went on rummaging the content of the bags. Our efforts were absolutely pointless. We returned to the hus and carefully barred the door. Szymon put his magnum gun on the table – just to be on the safe side. We had to go back to our usual household activities. And so half the day went by. The bear was still there, and only the shuffling on gravel pebbles made us aware of his presence. We did not disturb each other. It was an interesting experience. Not everybody can boast of having a bear in their backyard. We warned our real guests from Werenhus through the radio not to come too early. They only arrived at Hyttevika in the afternoon. By then, the bear had moved onto one of the nearby rocks. He was engorged with the food consumed at his litter feast and felt too heavy to walk on. He stayed there until the next morning, then he disappeared and did not come back again.

On a daily basis we were surrounded by other, less exciting, animals. I got especially attached to the little auks that were swarming on the slopes just behind Hyttevika hut. These small Arctic 'penguins', that's often what they're called because of their black and white feathers, would not let us forget about their presence. Day or night, midnight or noon, we were constantly surrounded by their piercing screams. We woke up and went to sleep accompanied by the auks' voices. These tiny winged beasts were never tired. Whole flocks would restlessly and relentlessly hover over our heads and make innumerable circles around us. The little auks were ubiquitous. Their presence became an inseparable element of our presence at Hyttevika. Their shrill hubbub and hustle and bustle accompanied our everyday life in the hus. Later, at the end of August, the auks left their Arctic dominion and flew south. When we were walking at the foot of the mountains, which had held their colonies, we missed their noisy and winged company. A calm set in. It was not disturbed by birds' cries. Everything seemed lifeless. It was a certain harbinger of winter. But for most of our stay in Hyttevika the rocky slopes and the sky above us were full of life and commotion.

I really liked watching reindeer. Quite a lot of them were grazing nearby. They never came in herds, usually just small groups of two or three. We often saw females with their young, who never squandered the chance to suckle their mother's milk. Some of the 'babies' still walked awkwardly on their disproportionately long legs. At other times, we came across lone males with antlers like the branches of a huge old tree. They must have been long in the tooth. Irrespective of their age, reindeers are all equally likeable. They are a bit smaller than their Siberian relatives, more stocky and have thicker fur. Thanks to that they are more resistant to cold. They seem very trusting and usually you can approach them very closely. They will look at you with their big dark eyes, as if surprised at the sight of you, and then will return to plucking their tundra treats. There is something hilarious and comforting at the same time in the way they run, throwing their lopsided legs apart.

Except for the little auks and reindeer, we also had other inseparable companions in the hus' closest neighbourhood. They were Arctic foxes otherwise known as polar foxes. There were five of them, which were really friendly and came up close to the hut. Four had coats of tundra colours: brown, dark brown and beige, and one was completely different, all black. It is a bit of an exaggeration to say that they were tame, but they certainly got used to our presence. Foxes have an extremely sociable and playful personality. It seemed to us that they were coming up just to show us how they played, fought and hunted, and whatever else their funny leaps could mean. They would hop and jump, prowl about, chase one another and coil themselves. They were cheering us up with their tricks and stunts. If it hadn't been for our duties, we could have been observing their habits and boisterous capering for hours. However, the way we got acquainted with Hyttevika foxes was quite a different story. It did not look so funny at the beginning.

In the morning, when the stove had gone cold in the night and there was no warm water, we used to go to the stream for a quick wash. The water temperature was 0.5°C, the fact of which was announced to us by the hydrogeologists who were conducting research in the area. But in the morning such fresh water coming from the ice resources from the ground was perfect to wake you up. Our 'washing post' or 'water drawing stand' was so compact that it could be used only by one person at a time.

'I left you the soap by the stream,' announced Szymon on his way back from our 'streamlined bathroom'.

'All right, thanks. I'll go there in a sec, must finish yesterday's notes,' I was doing my best not to lag behind with my diary notes.

Unfortunately, my scrupulousness was to blame for the loss of our only bar of soap. When after a couple of minutes I reached the stream, there was not a sign of the soap or a soap dish. But in the vicinity I could see a fox trotting up and down the place.

'Fox! It's you. You are the guilty one!' We ran after the rascal hoping to find our lost items. We followed the fox as he was the only suspect visible in the area.

'He must have taken them to play. They must be lying around here somewhere.'

Our search ended with a qualified success. We came across only the soap dish. The soap itself sank like a stone.

'It's just impossible that it vanished into thin air!'

'Maybe the fox gulped it down? We've already heard stories about the bear who was feasting on washing powder, why shouldn't the fox try some soap? This white thing with a peculiar smell might turn out to be a tasty morsel.'

'We'll have to keep an eye on the foxes in case one of them goes foamy…'

But none of them did. The puzzle remained unsolved and we were left with no soap at all.

'Well, we'll have to go to Werenhus, cap in hand, and beg for some.' But that had to be put off for later. First our day's field work had to be done. Just in case we left a note in the hus reading as follows: 'The foxes have devoured our soap. Help!' As if every Spitsbergen wanderer going past Hyttevika was carrying a bar of soap to spare.

To our surprise, when we came back home after a few good hours, we found an elegant brand new bar of soap on the table. Good spirits of Werenhus were not idle. Accidentally, Jasiu, the resident of Werenhus, was walking by Hyttevika hut while doing his field work, dropped in to make some tea and read our desperate plea for help. Then Czarek ('Tschaarek') and Bartek were coming from Werenhus to Hyttevika depot for fresh supplies as not everything had been carried to Werenhus yet. It was they who brought us the soap. We rejoiced over it! Such joy at a simple piece of soap. But that was not all. We were happy to have invisible helpers whose assistance was so tangible. We were delighted with their goodwill and selfless help. Even if it was just a trifle, it was something important to us.

Life in the hus reminds you of existence on a desert island. You must cope with various problems, but you are limited to the things you have around you. It also brings to mind a comparison to prehistoric times, with its distinct division into male and female roles.

'I'm going to chop some wood,' declared Szymon, and then for half the day you could hear the rhythmical beat of the axe blows. Small logs and spills were piling up against the house walls. We still had some supplies, which either had been brought by the Norwegians, or were of local origin: the driftwood we picked up on the shore. In this ice-and-rock world, where the trees do not grow higher than a couple of centimetres, we burnt wood from Siberian taiga. We brought chopped logs in buckets to the hus and stacked them by the stove and in the hallway. Just to have a reserve and also for those who would come here after us. This is the unwritten code of the hus. Everything that is superfluous or redundant, everything that you can easily get in the South after your return home – you leave for its future occupants. You never know under what circumstances someone may reach this place. You never know your luck, some day this heap of surplus wood may save someone's life.

During Szymon's manly struggle with the wood I took up traditionally female jobs. I went between the hut and the stream several times carrying buckets of water, patiently filling up a big pot on the stove. After a few hours the water would be boiling and ready to use for our evening meal, washing up the dishes and for a hot bath in a wooden tub. The tub is made up of several planks and a plastic sheet lining it inside.

I swept the floor. It turned out to be quite a hard task. If you take into consideration the number of cracks, slits and gaps in the wooden floor, you can imagine the amount of sand and filth that gets stuck in there. I cleaned the stove. I never thought this dirty work was going to please me so much. I looked at my accomplishment with immense satisfaction. But when you are in the North, you are no longer surprised at the fact that some values have been redefined. There is no time to complicate matters, which seems to be an inborn human inclination. It is the basic things that guarantee your survival here. How do you suppose you could make it in the Arctic without the stove being in a good working order?

Most of the days are spent on field work. Taking advantage of good weather, we worked for more than ten hours collecting research material. Then we carried out our household chores in the hus. Very late in the evening – if you can say so in relation to white nights full of sunshine – finally came the time for rest. We sat down on the wooden doorstep of the hut. Before us there was a narrow strip of colourful gravel beach. The sea had been polishing these rock chips for thousands of years, turning them into beautifully rounded pebbles. Further on there was the boundless waters of the Greenland Sea. The waves slightly changed the configuration of the beach chippings every time they came in. A magnificent spectacle that we watched every day from the threshold of our home.

Today we have a new attraction. The east wind has blown numerous icebergs from the further part of the fjord. After a few warm days the glaciers started to melt intensively and the glacier fronts began to break off. You shouldn't be surprised at such a big gathering of them in the sea. But we are astonished at the multitude of various forms and shapes, colours and shades, sizes, sounds and movements. They float majestically on the waters of the 'Home Bay' or freeze in their tracks – massive white giants and smaller crystal clear ice blocks, which broke off some glacier and have already melted considerably. Among them you can see light and dark blue lumps or blocks of ice reminding you of any figure or object your imagination can conjure up.

'Just look at this beautiful swan!'

'Come on, it's not a swan. It's a sailing boat, a real three-master. And next to it, look! A hippo.'

'Yeah, with open jaws. He is about to swallow this tiny ice duck in front of him.'

The game involving the icebergs and our imaginations could last a long time. We have similar fun while observing the clouds, which can be very changeable and in the strong Arctic wind may assume various fanciful shapes. Very often we do not say anything. We just sit on the doorstep of our hus. We gaze at the sea – in the middle of the night. The icebergs are lit by a low northern sun. Calm. Only untiring little auks continue their shrill crying. But in some sense they are also an element of this Arctic peace and quiet. We are silent. There are no words to express such undisturbed tranquillity.

❀   ❀   ❀

From the diary of my third stay in Spitsbergen:

Krzysiek ('Ksheeshek') came by boat to Hyttevika port to collect our luggage. The loading, talks and arrangements took quite a while – I decided to use that time to look inside the hut. I had not dropped in there even once that year. The present inhabitants of Hyttevika, geologists from Cracow, had left the hut for a couple of days to do some field work. The shutters were closed on the windows and it was completely dark inside. I went in with a candle in my hand. I could not see anything at first. Gradually, the contours of objects came out of the darkness. I tried to recognise the items which I used when I lived there three years before. I came across familiar pots, the same old kettle with a fancifully curved long spout, the same small bowls and completely new mugs. To my dismay, I could not recollect the previous ones, the ones we had used before. Another unpleasant discovery was a new bigger coal stove installed by the Cracow people. A small pot-bellied stove with an intricate design on its grating, which I liked so much, was disconnected and put aside. There were also a lot of 'strange' belongings and luggage lying around. This was the property of other people who called Hyttevika their home… My eyes slowly got accustomed to semi-darkness and the interior of Hyttevika emerged from blackness – before my eyes and in my memories (…).

Hyttevika destroyed by a polar bear.

9 Time and changes

The content of the experienced time shrunk and expanded in turns,
in the way that made your head dizzy.
You could express it in a few words, but almost immediately
it would swell in your conscience to some undefined dimensions,
which all words were helpless to express.

Jan Jozef Szczepanski, *The Polar Bear Bay*

During one of our excursions in the locality of Werenhus we decided to make for the most westward end of Elveflya, the vast flatland created by deposits brought by glacial rivers. We wanted to reach Pyttholmen – the biggest island on that part of the coast. Our friend Pepa, the leader of the Czech explorers, told us so much about it that we wanted to see its beauty with our own eyes. He also assured us that we could actually walk there, instead of going by boat. The only thing we had to do was to choose the right moment of low tide. Indeed, after a long march on a monotonous gravel plain we approached the vicinity of our destination, and we found no boundary between the dry land marked on the map and the sea basin. Instead, there was a wide area stretching in front of us, strewn with hundreds of small rock hills. The lows between them were filled with shallow water or black muddy silt. The tide was out. In this part of Spitsbergen the tidal range can be almost two metres. What we can see now is the sea bed, which has temporarily emerged from the water. The rock hills turn out to be skerries. Normally, they are hidden just under the water surface and pose a great danger to boats and ships. We do not ponder long.

We can see the outline of the land and some higher rocks in the distance. It must be Pyttholmen! But it does not look like an island now. It seems to be within our grasp. Pepa was right. Curiosity spurs us into action. But as the proverb goes: 'Curiosity killed the cat'.

I never thought before that walking on the sea bottom could be so easy! There are a lot of skerries and they are located so close to one another that they form a kind of pavement. We walk on it with no problem at all, as the surface of the rocks is flat and wide. They resemble wide domes. That is the result of forces exerted by former glaciers, which polished and smoothed all irregularities on the rocks. We meticulously avoid treacherous muddy hollows and jump from one rock to another. The distance to the 'island' is quickly getting shorter.

We have finally reached it. We can feel the difference under our feet. The ground is much more stable here. We walk around the island. It is quite small so the walk does not take too much time. In its central part there is a lake, which is a feeding place for various birds. Next to the lake there are fabulous rocks. Tall and slim, twisted at different angles, cracked and weathered – they have fanciful shapes resembling the soaring towers and pointy turrets of medieval castles or cathedrals, lashed by the sea waves now. A most unusual place. We feel it's magic even more when we realise that in fact we are on a desert island. We mustn't forget about the tide! For the time being, however, we relish the loveliness and tranquillity of this newly discovered beauty spot. We make ourselves comfortable behind one of the rocks, admiring a beautiful view over the lake. It's an ideal place to do bird watching. It is a perfect bird sanctuary. You can see barnacle geese, ptarmigans, eiders and sandpipers. How calmly and gracefully they move! Idyllic surroundings. Czarek ('Tchaarek') takes out some chocolate from his rucksack – a dessert on a desert island. After a while Bartek ('Bhartek') leaves us and goes in search of some privacy. But he runs back in no time at all.

'Gee! Let's get out of here!' Bartek was panting as he explained what had happened. 'I went around that rock over there and what did I see? No skerries! All our skerries are gone!'

We jumped to our feet in panic and climbed the nearby hill. It was a fact. Little ponds and mud in the hollows disappeared as well as most of our skerry bridge. It was all flooded except for the highest rocks. We couldn't see any big tidal waves coming in, but we could definitely see how the dry area of the rocky ground was shrinking. The tide was cutting us off from the land. Pyttholmen was becoming an island again. Between us and the dry land there were no longer any rock hills, but tiny islands gradually disappearing under the tidal waters. The landscape was changing before our very eyes.

Rocky pillars at Pyttholmen.

At first, we were overcome with amazement mixed with fascination for the phenomenon we were witnessing.

'Is it really that quick?! How long have we been here?! Half an hour? In such a short time such tidewater?!' Each of us was aware of the principles ruling the tides, but we were completely taken by surprise. We did not expect events to progress so speedily.

Then we felt a surge of panic.

'What shall we do now? Shall we try and go back?'

'Maybe it's better to wait? In six hours the tide will be out again.'

'Yeah … but we have nothing to eat, besides, they will be dead worried in Werenhus. It was supposed to be a short outing…'

'I suggest we go back. After all, not all the skerries have been covered by the water yet. We should be able to make it. But we must hurry. The sooner we do it, the better.'

So, it was decided. We are going back. But this time we are going to cross the sea and not walk on land. The distance between the island and dry land seems to be much longer than before on our way here. It looked as if we were stuck there for good. It was waders that saved our lives. Each of us had a pair of them in our rucksacks. We used them to cross the Glacier River behind Werenhus that morning. The water there was reaching up to our thighs in some places. I don't want to think what would have happened if we had left those boots on the riverbank as we usually did. Usually we put them into plastic bags, rolled a stone or two over them and left them by the riverside so as not to have to carry them around. I do not know why we took the waders with us that day. Normal wellington boots would not have been sufficient. In the last four metres before the dry land the water reached above our knees. Walking became extremely difficult as the water was quite resistant. We could not see the bumpy ground beneath our feet because we were making the water muddy and cloudy. But we managed to reach the land. Exhausted from physical effort and adrenaline, we flopped down on the stable ground. At that moment we had no doubt we were on the edge of the shore and that Pyttholmen was an island indeed.

We were taken by surprise by the passage of time and changes in the world around us. But we expected those changes, we were aware of them and took them into consideration while planning the return. However, when they came, we did not recognise that they were already happening. We did not suspect that the reality could change so much and so quickly in such a short time. In the days to come, we were to see again and again how relative is the notion of the flow of time as well as constancy and changeability in the Arctic world.

In recent years the issue of climate change has become very topical. The example of retreating glaciers in polar areas and the quick pace of such changes is given as one of the key arguments for the existence of global warming. It is a fact that the range of most glaciers has decreased. In order to see that, however, you must look at the photographs taken at least a couple of years ago or more. These 'dramatic' changes do not happen overnight and cannot be noticed on a daily basis. But there are other places that astound you by their dynamics of change. If you happen to be there day by day, you may not recognise the area you saw the day before. These are the forefields of the glaciers – the grounds that have just emerged from underneath the ice masses retreating inland. In some sense, it is a new face of the Earth, which is being formed after awakening from her long sleep of some hundreds or even thousands years under a thick ice blanket. Now she is waking up. She regains her freedom. But she has not gained her final shape yet – she is still changing, trying on various 'outfits', as if to see which one suits her best. Hence the constant movement, matching, formation – the process of creation is still going on. Nowhere else in the Arctic does the landscape change so fast. In this respect, the forefields of glaciers are fascinating. In spite of this fact, they might seem a very ugly and hostile area.

One such place was situated just behind Werenhus. Just behind its walls there was a lateral moraine bank of the Werenskiold glacier. The embankment constituted some kind of boundary between two entirely different worlds. On the one side, there were old rock surfaces covered with a thick layer of moss and lichen, looking unmoved and motionless. On the other side, just behind the moraine bank, there was chaotic scenery, in colours of grey and black, full of innumerable, big and small pointy hills, mounds and banks made of muddy loam or apparently solid rock material. But if you try to climb them, loose chippings fall from underneath your feet and immediately scatter and shower down. Under the thin cover of the rocky rubble you can see the glitter of the crystal-clear ice. It is the last proof of the glacier's activity and presence in this area. Now it is just dead ice blocks buried under the stony deposits.

New land emerging from beneath the retreating glacier – grey and lifeless moraine at the Werenskiold Glacier foreland.

Immense spring at the Werenskiold Glacier foreland.

Ice and mud – the moraine at the Werenskiold Glacier foreland.

Morainic hilly landscape.

Among the icy and rocky hills there are numerous ponds, streams and hollows, sometimes having amazingly regular shapes. They remind you of lunar craters but they are just traces of ice blocks that melted away quite recently. How much of the ice is left underneath the stony surface? How many times will moraine hills and mounds collapse – burying the ponds and changing the course of the streams? How long will it take – the whole process of melting the ice blocks and creating a new world?

Everything is soaked with water. Your feet get bogged down in the mud or get stuck in the slush made up of water, ice and stones. In several places the water gushes out and up creating impressive bubbling fountains. They resemble geysers or boiling water, or rather boiling mud, as the transparency of the liquid is far from that of clear water. A massive amount of fine mineral material carried from the glacier gives brownish grey hue, reminding you of the colour of white coffee. It does however provide some variety from the dominant black and grey shades. In other places of the forefield there is crystal-clear water in the small moraine lakes. They are so shallow that after a few days of sunshine they warm up to such an extent you can bathe there.

Forms of life are barely visible. Only here and there, in the part of the forefield that is the furthest away from the glacier, do the first plants appear. Some moss, lichen, blue-green algae, sometimes single clumps of saxifrages. Apart from that, it is a desert, as if life is keeping a low profile and still waiting. Waiting for the unstable surface to settle down, stabilise and take on its final form. However, the most fascinating thing for me is the very changeability and variability of forms and shapes, which surprise you every time you enter the maze of moraine – it's virtually impossible to find anywhere that is unchanged.

'What a gloomy landscape! Just stones and mud. And everything is so dark. How can you say this place is charming?' My family are looking at the photos and making highly critical comments about Werenskiold forefield. I do understand them. The charm of this place cannot be rendered in the photographs. Its beauty lies in its dynamics, in a continuous change, alteration and transformation. But isn't that also true of human life?

The Arctic scenery can also display the complete opposite of changeability, an amazing stability and durability of some forms, as if they were untouched by the passage of time. The most unusual thing, in my opinion, is the remains of the road along the northern coast of Hornsund.

'Look at these ruts made by car wheels. How come they are here?' The fact that there were tracks in such virgin territory was most surprising. They just weren't in harmony with that unspoiled nature. I was quite astonished when I saw them for the first time around the base. They were distinct, parallel ruts cut in the stony and mossy surface. They indicated the route of some wheeled vehicle.

'Yes, these are the tracks of a car,' my astonishment seemed misplaced to the old regulars of Hornsund, 'it used to drive this way very often. This route along the shoreline was the shortest way to reach the sub-base Hyttevika and Wroclaw Baranowka ('Vrotslove Bharanoovka') from the Polar Station of Polish Academy of Sciences.'

'But I haven't seen any car at the base. There is only a tractor and PTS boats but they leave different traces. Besides that, I thought you were not allowed to drive any cars since the establishment of the national park in this area. You are only exempt from this regulation in the closest vicinity of the base. But now I have seen these tracks…'

'Yes, you are right. The last jeep drove this way over thirty years ago. It carried the building materials for the construction of Baranowka hut. After that the road was not used again.'

Over thirty years ago? But the ruts cut into delicate tundra look so fresh, as if they were only made yesterday. The scars inflicted by one of the foremost inventions of our civilisation cut deeply into nature's body. In many places, along the coastline, the clearly visible fragments of the old road have been preserved. We passed by them quite often on our way between the base and Werenhus. Tundra grows slowly and any damage it sustains can be long lasting, even permanent, as if time has no healing power over its injuries. The durability of the road ruts is like a reproach for the incautious actions and aspirations of our civilisation.

Traces of an old road remain in the fragile Arctic environment.

The course of time may take yet another form in the Arctic – a form of an apparent permanence and immutability. However, it is only our human perspective that does not let us notice the continuous change of nature.

We often walk along the shoreline between the Station of Polish Academy of Sciences and Werenhus hut. Even an amateur who is not an expert in earth science can clearly see flat areas, creating some step-like formations, cascading from the mountain slopes down to the sea. They are of different widths and lengths. Some variety is added to them by isolated rocks. In some places there are several such terraces, elsewhere there are dozens. They seem to be a lasting and unchanged element of the landscape in this area but you couldn't be more wrong. Each level represents movement. The wide flat areas elevated now to the height of several dozen metres above the sea level used to be beaches. Under the moss cover you can find rounded pebbles, the effect of the industrious activity of sea waves that took place some thousands of years ago. Single rocks protruding out of the flat area, which serve us now as road signs on our way to Werenhus, are former skerries. Their shapes resemble closely those still immersed in

Ideally rounded pebbles on the raised beaches.

the water. But who knows what is going to happen in the next several thousand years? Maybe these picturesque small islands scattered off the coast will also get elevated far above the water? The process continues. The land is still rising. We do not notice that. In our human timescale we see only stability and permanence. May it remain that way. We need them after all as a counterbalance to our fascination with change and movement.

A similar thing can be said about the mountains in Spitsbergen. You admire the soaring jagged ridges from afar. They represent the idea of durability, unchangeability and eternity – the symbols usually associated with rocks and mountains. But as you climb suddenly everything becomes loose and unstable. Their slopes are covered with a thick layer of weathered rock debris. Each step may trigger a rock avalanche. Subsequent rocks and stones slide down when stepped upon. The ground is dangerously unstable. The massif, the bedrock, turns out to be extremely brittle on the surface. It is just an impermanent heap of rock chips and chunks. Mountains are getting old too. They are falling apart or going to pieces. Everything is changing – even the symbol of permanence.

Some changes go unnoticed when they are happening, but after some time we suffer their consequences. The silting of Nottinghambukta – a wide bay in the vicinity of Werenhus – is a good example. A lot of senior explorers still remember that they transported goods to Wroclaw ('Vrotslove') hut by boat. You could go far into the bay and unload all the commodities nearby the hut. However, those days are over. The rivers flowing out of the glaciers are constantly bringing more deposits into the sea. The delta is growing while the bay is becoming shallower. Subsequent ports in natural small bays along the coastline are silting up. They have to be abandoned as the boats get bogged down in the mud. The unloading takes place in ports located more and more towards the sea. In recent years, fewer and fewer boats are going into Nottinghambukta, even to the furthest port. The unloading for Werenhus is done at Hyttevika now, from where there is still a half-hour march to Werenhus. We actually feel this environmental change in our muscles, while carrying loads and walking several times along once-rocky, once-muddy roads. The change does not occur abruptly. There are no dramatic developments or spectacular natural disasters. But in an indirect way we are painfully affected by it.

Other changes have their own cyclic rhythm. We learn about it, for instance, when crossing the rivers that flow from the glaciers. Just behind Werenhus there is the Glacier River coming from Werenskiold glacier. We had a chance to observe its habits on a regular basis. In the morning, we had no problem crossing it. There was very little water and we could easily walk on the stony river bed, just in our wellies. But in the afternoon, especially on a warm and sunny day, when the glacier melted

Crossing a glacial river is a big challenge!

intensively, the same place would turn out to be a barrier you couldn't break through. The water sometimes reaches above your thighs. Even hip waders may be too short. The current gets so strong that putting each step forward in the river becomes a great battle with the elements. Without the support of the trekking poles or holding hands with other people, you have no chance of crossing the white water. The rapids do not allow you to lift your foot in the first place, and then, if you are lucky enough to do so, they take advantage of your momentary weakness and attack with redoubled fury. It is difficult to keep your balance, especially standing on one foot. At some spots the river current is so powerful that making any move in any direction seems impossible. But, think about the fact that, in a few hours, this rushing water element will turn into a peaceful shallow stream again.

From the diary of my third stay in Spitsbergen:

> *It is the third time I have spent my summer here, in Spitsbergen. Once more I had a chance to sail onto the cool waters of Hornsund. Once again I could return to the cosy wooden walls of Werenhus. I'm coming back here, as if coming back home.*

Each time it gets more and more natural. The first moments inside – I look around and into every nook and cranny. Everything looks the same. My friend – the table. A good old table with its slanting top, reinforced with boards on all edges but one – to allow the breadcrumbs to be swept away. The same stove that helped me three years ago to make friends with Werenhus and get accustomed to it. There is a familiar dark-coloured fleece blanket folded on the bench. It was made by my mum before my first expedition and brought here by me. There are some tea towels that came here likewise. I find my favourite mug in the cupboard – it has the picture of two teddy bears and an inscription in Czech 'Miláčkovi' ('Meelhatchkovee') which means more or less that the mug is dedicated 'To Cuddly Kiddie - My Love'. There is the same clock on the wall, which was made by Szymon two years ago. He cut out a slate, engraved digits on it and painted them silver. The clock has altered a little bit. A fragment of the schist broke off. The four o'clock suffered slightly. This small change drew my attention. It was quite symbolic that it was the clock, the indicator of time, which changed. It was the only thing that registered the changes … Later, I also discovered some time-worn colourful mugs, which I had bought with my friend Anka ('Ahnka') in one of the Wroclaw ('Vrotslove') supermarkets only two years ago. Some of the mugs showed wear and tear, they were chipped and one handle broke off. They were probably nearing their 'timeout'. Time … The time in Spitsbergen passes in a strange way. On the one hand, it seems that time does not exist at all. On the other hand, everything is different each time you go there.

I haven't been here for two years. When we reached the port in Hornsund and I went ashore, it turned out that there were a lot of my friends at the base, to whom I had said goodbye exactly two years ago. Now I'm greeting them again. There is the whole technical team present as well as the boys who were staying for the winter when I was leaving. Now they are spending the summer here or are going to winter here again. There are also other people I met two or three years ago. All these familiar faces I met during my different expeditions have merged together and become condensed into one time – they exist here and now. Hence the feeling I'm coming back home – to my family and friends. It seems as if these two years of my absence here did not take place at all. I feel as if nothing really happened between 'yesterday', in those two years, and 'today', the present time. The real space and time have disappeared. Time has stopped. It is as though I boarded the ship to go away only yesterday. I love warm welcomes on the shores *of Hornsund. They are so cordial and moving even if you shake hands with people whom you don't know well, whose faces you only just remember. But they are a part of this Polish corner and Polish 'homeland' at the North Pole. Even if we have no contact with one another back at home, in Poland – we belong to different worlds, places, generations, vocations – we feel the authentic and sincere joy at meeting one another. We are united by our common interest in Spitsbergen and the time we spend together in the Arctic. Time that obeys only its own rules, which goes by at its own pace. (…)*

But changes do happen. In spite of the fact that I see the same places, find the same objects and paths, meet my old friends, I must finally accept that there are more changes than long-lasting things. I have changed, too. People are different – even the people I knew before. In a different line-up of the expedition team their behaviour changes. What used to be funny, now it is not. What used to be discussed is now obsolete. The whole atmosphere of Werenhus is dissimilar. It is not only a matter of a chipped stone clock or dilapidated mugs. Even the tundra is less flowery and colourful this year. Little auks are more silent in our neighbourhood. I wrote about my feelings in the Werenhus Book before my departure:

'It's the third time I've spent my summer in Spitsbergen … I'm glad I have been given one more chance to go back. To feel the vast Arctic space. When you return to Werenhus, you feel on the one hand that the time has stopped. You see the same kitchen objects, the table and the chairs. The same wooden roof in the attic when you open your eyes in the morning. The same views and paths you followed many times before. But at the same time, each stay here is different. Werenhus reveals its different faces. The place is seemingly the same, but something intangible and indefinable in the atmosphere of this house changes every year. New people, new encounters – new composition of our Wroclaw expeditions and new guests crossing the threshold of the hut. That is the greatest magic of this place, the permanence and stability of the home on the other hand contrasted with the constant changes brought by each person who comes here. Each of us takes their own individual memories of this unique place located at the end of the world – our little cosy Werenhus.'

In the world of human emotions and feelings nothing is set forever. And it is not only the external circumstances that influence us. It is also ourselves who, through mutual relations with other people and the world, create stability or bring about changes. It is we who decide at what pace our time will pass.

Lake on Pyttholmen island; looking towards mainland and Naan Glacier.

The clock in Werenhus.

10 Glaciers

An expedition to Torell Glacier had been planned for a long time. We were supposed to collect samples of water from warm karst springs for chemical analysis by our befriended hydrogeologists. We were also going to take food supplies to our Czech speleologists, who under Pepa's leadership were planning further exploration of ice caves later in the autumn. Additionally, Szymon ('Sheemon') wanted to take that opportunity to register in the GPS system an exact location of all skerries in the bay before the glacier front. He was working upon a navigation map at that time. The expedition had quite a lot of tasks on the agenda. We were only waiting for good weather to set in.

Finally, the weather forecast was favourable and the situation was supposed to be stable for at least several hours or so. Having packed all necessary equipment and food supplies, we set off for one of the natural ports – a small bay where our boat was moored. I was extremely excited about the expedition as I had been looking forward to it for ages. After all, we were heading for the biggest glacier in that area of Spitsbergen. I was to see the famous Torell Glacier. What's more, I was to see

The impressive ice front of the Torell Glacier.

outflows of warm water (so-called resurgences), which never freeze, in spite of the fact that they are located next to the massive body of the glacier. They were really something unique. In the whole area of Spitsbergen hot springs occur in very few places.

My enthusiasm ended very quickly when confronted with the bay silt. As we were going to map all the skerries, we had to set out at the lowest tide possible in order to see the rocks above the water surface or just beneath it. The low tide meant, however, that our boat got bogged down in the muddy shallows. Natural ports in Nottighambukta had practically ceased to serve their purpose. It was possible to use them only at high tide. We had to push the boat out of the silt and leave the bay at the lowest tide. It looked as if we had taken leave of our senses. It might not have been such a demanding task to complete if we had not been wearing survival suits, so called 'helly hansens' which combine a hood, jacket, gloves, trousers and wellington boots in one outfit. Such waterproof and anatomically shaped 'bags' were to protect our bodies against exposure. They were very baggy, especially mine. I had borrowed it from the base. The problem was that they had not provided suits in small women's sizes. I looked and felt like an astronaut walking in a spacesuit that was three or four sizes too big. It wouldn't have been a big problem if I had only been sitting in that 'straitjacket' in the boat. But moving in it was a completely different story. Especially as I was standing in water that reached up to my knees, and was trying to push the boat out of the mud. I had to do it on my own as Szymon was trying to start the engine. We had to coordinate both those actions at the same time. As for me, every step was leading to disaster. The 'wellies' of the suit, far too big for me, were getting stuck in the silt. At my attempt to move forward, my foot was slipping out of the boot, I was losing my balance and was grabbing hold of the boat side. Many times I was unsuccessful and ended up in the water with a big splash. It was a hopeless battle with the mud and oversized suit. The feeling of utter helplessness caused anger, in spite of all my efforts to stay calm. But the only thing I could do was grit my teeth and go on.

It took us approximately an hour and a half to successfully start the boat and take it out of the bay. My dream expedition had only just started and I was already so tired that I had no energy to enjoy it. Luckily, new impressions allowed me to soon forget the negative emotions from the unfortunate beginning of the journey. I had to concentrate on the next job. Sitting in the bow I was looking out for rocky obstacles in the sea bottom, as not everything could be seen clearly from the position of the steersman. We had to be extremely careful not to crash our boat. We were entering the realm of skerries. I had no idea there were so many of them so far off the coast. The low tide revealed a totally new underwater world of rocks. We were going very slowly. Our route was being registered by the GPS. Every now and then, we made some stops at bigger skerries to measure the exact coordinates of their location. It was very unusual to get off the boat in the middle of the sea. The tops of the rocks were just a little bit above the water. If somebody was watching us from the distance, they would have got the impression we were walking on the sea's surface!

The mapping of skerries was finally finished and we could proceed further.

'So, shall we go near the front of the glacier? You surely want to have a closer look at Torell?' I don't have to say anything, Szymon already knows my answer and steers the boat towards a massive ice barrier materialising in front of us. With every metre it gets bigger and bigger.

'We shouldn't go any closer. A block of ice can break off any second. Even this distance is a bit risky. The wave brought about by breaking the ice would without doubt shower the boat. But today calving of the glacier shouldn't be so intense.' Szymon looks with his expert eye at the ice surface and cloudy sky. 'It is cool today and calving is first of all affected by high temperature and sunshine. But we must be careful, anyway. Glaciers are quite unpredictable, but you are well aware of that yourself.'

I just nod my head and can't take my eyes of the rising wall of ice just in front of me.

'Well, I didn't expect it to be so gigantic…' My imagination could not comprehend the figures: Torell – surface of 488 square kilometres, height of the glacier front from 60 to 80 metres. I couldn't visualise it. Now I understand. This is a giant. It commands respect. My fascination with its mighty power is mixed with fear.

The ice barrier is not uniform. When observed from far away, from the shore, it seems to be a smooth line marking out the boundary between the sea and ice but when closer, it is seen to be indented and winding. In some places the water cuts deeply into the ice with bays, in other places it retreats – ice peninsulas and promontories go far out into the sea. With each successive recess, the cliffs reveal before our eyes countless nooks, niches, cornices, needles, arcades, towers and pillars. All of them elaborately carved out of the ice by the sun, rain, wind and waves. Over our heads, just at the top of the glacier front, there is a real ice ridge with lofty jagged peaks – impossible to conquer. It resembles the white crests of the stormy waves suddenly frozen and stopped in their motion. Most of these giant but fragile forms are bent or twisted in all possible directions, as if they have left Hundertwasser's or Gaudi's artistic studios. The apparent avoidance of straight lines twists ice pillars and columns, makes folds of them, bends down towers like weary heads. In some places there's the impression that the glacier head is tilted towards us. The glacier looks as if it is tensing itself, preparing to leap and attack us.

A rich diversity of shapes is complemented by the different shades. There is seemingly only a white and sky-blue colour. But the play of light and shadows – the semi-darkness of narrow bays and the diffused light of a cloudy sky – paint every recess, crack or niche in their own unique shade. Blue occurs in tens of hues, in different tones and saturation. Even white appears to have various degrees of whiteness. The further the boat moves, the more is unfolded. A beautiful spectacle of form and colour. Majesty and mightiness. I can't think of better words to describe this colossus of ice. All expressions seem feeble in relation to this giant. Our boat looks like a nutshell juxtaposed with its hugeness. But this tiny boat is the only safe haven for us now. At least we choose to believe so.

'That's the end of the sightseeing tour. We must go on. It's still a long way ahead. And some work to do.' Suddenly I heard the voice of reason. It wasn't mine and it was speaking to me.

'Pity … Shall we come here again on our way back? Please…' I felt unsatisfied and was hungry for more.

'We'll see. It depends on the sea conditions. Can't promise you that. But maybe we can get into one of Torell's ice caves. They are just next to the hot springs and we will be going in that direction. I hope the entrances are still there. I haven't been to that place since last autumn. A lot of things could have changed, you know…'

Our peaceful and idyllic drifting in front of Torell came to an end. Ahead of us lay the most difficult part of our expedition. We had to go up a wide glacial river, against its extremely strong current and through numerous whirlpools. The engine was working in top gear. We were supposed to enter the rushing rapids of the river at high speed to avoid capsizing. I am not sure if I fully understood the gravity of the situation then, but it was better that way. There was no time to consider all the pros and cons. We had to act quickly and decisively. My actions were limited to balancing the boat with my body. The main responsibility lay with the steersman. But looking at Szymon's face, so concentrated and focused on the task, and knowing his previous experience with ice-cold waters of the Greenland Sea, I was confident that our risky ride would end well.

'Hold on tight! Watch out! Here we go into the main stream of the white water!' Further words were drowned out by the roaring of the muddy brown water going straight against our bow. It attacked our boat. I felt a powerful blow. The boat turned a bit but we were still making our way up the river. Several more times, the fast-flowing current tugged the boat unmercifully and pulled her into the midst of the pitched battle. We fought off subsequent assaults. There was no time to feel terror or despair. Only much later, when I looked back on it, did I fully realise how dangerous that situation had been.

Finally, we had to stop the boat somehow. Szymon made a more abrupt turn towards the river bank and one powerful blow of the current fired us, as if from a catapult, onto land. At least I thought it was land. Still excited and feeling all the adrenaline of our crazy ride I got off the boat and sank up to my knees in the muddy ground. This time it was not silt but gravels mixed with slush. We landed on the moraine – the limitless chaotic space, full of rocks, stones, loose chippings, gravels, sand, fine dust and loam. And all that soaked with water. A very tricky mixture. We were supposed to walk on such ground for the rest of our journey.

We did our best to anchor the boat as safely as possible on the moving ground. Then we set off towards Raudfjellet, the mountain range, at the foot of which hot springs were located. After my struggle with the silt in the bay I was convinced that the worst part was behind me. I should have known better. Walking in an oversized helly-hansen suit on the 'marshy' moraine was even more demanding. It was killing me and I lagged far behind Szymon. My feet were getting stuck in the unstable surface and I kept tripping over my own suit. I must have looked ridiculous. I felt like sitting on the nearest rock, starting to cry and not walking one step further. But what purpose would that serve? After all, I did want to see the hot springs and ice caves. I had no option but to go on. I dragged my feet on that boggy ground, detesting that horrible suit more and more. Finally, I decided to take it off. What a relief! I preferred to carry a heavy and cumbersome bundle than torment myself with wearing it. I'd like to have left it next to some rock and retrieved it on my way back, but I couldn't do that. A polar bear could have been interested in it. You can't possibly go on the boat on the ice-cold Arctic waters without a survival suit. Whether I wanted it or not, I had to carry it with me.

The reddish slopes of the Raudfjellet did not seem to be getting any nearer. The same was true of the lateral wall of Torell Glacier. It ended on the land and closed the horizon on the right-hand side. It wasn't getting any closer. I had already covered such a long distance and the mountain was still so remote. I must have been wrong in my estimation of the Arctic distance. The transparency of the polar air makes everything look as if it is very near, which can be very misleading. Mountains or glaciers looming on the horizon seem to be within your grasp. You think you need an hour or so to reach them. Then, one hour extends to several hours and your target is still far away.

I was exhausted and weary of the monotony of the route.

But everything has its end in this world. In this case I should add the word: 'fortunately'. I finally made it. I reached the rocky walls of the Raudfjellet. Szymon had already managed to find a metal barrel with the Czech's supplies. He did a stocktake and left the fresh supplies.

'Fancy some chocolate? Or condensed milk? Some sugar will boost your energy.' I must have looked really poorly if I needed such care and concern.

I sat down and only then did I notice the aim of our expedition.

'It's so green around here. Incredible! And it's in the middle of the rocky desert just by the glacier.'

The narrow stretches of intense greenery were incongruous amongst the bare surroundings. They appeared out of the blue, in places where water warmed by the Earth's heat was gushing out of deep crevices onto the surface. The green 'belts' were meandering alongside shallow streams coming out of the springs. Then, after a couple of metres, the greenery was disappearing. At that distance the water probably cooled down so much that it wasn't able to support any life around it.

'What's interesting is that these springs don't freeze in the winter and it's still green all around them. We're at real thermal baths.'

'Yeah, in their Arctic variant.' The temperature measured by us was far from the 'normal' expectation for hot springs. It was not quite 11°C, but in Arctic conditions it was a sensational phenomenon. It created a green oasis of life at the heart of the ice and rock desert.

'Let's see one more curio,' Szymon got up and started to pack water samples into his rucksack, 'I managed to check that before you came. The entrances to the caves are accessible. We can go inside. Just a little bit, not too far. At this time of year it might be risky. In the summer the glacier is in its most active state, it is moving. Autumn is the best time to explore glacial caves when frost stabilises the ice. But you won't be here any longer in the autumn so you must be happy with this small grotto in Torell's side. You want to see it?

'Of course, I do. Let's go there now!' During all my stays in Spitsbergen I saw so many photos and films from the ice caves, and listened to so many stories about the fabulous world hidden inside the glaciers that obviously I could not miss the chance to see it myself.

We reached Torell Glacier quickly. The part of it coming onto land did not look as dangerous as the other side, which was cliff-like and ended abruptly in the sea. The glacier reminded you of an ice and snow dome gently meeting the ground. In one spot, the smooth surface of the wall was broken. A semi-circular, gate-like structure, resembling the portals of Romanesque churches, was leading deep into the massive body of the glacier. A wide tunnel was hidden behind a curtain of dripping water. At the entrance thousands of water drops were coming down from the melting ceiling of the glacier. A rapid shallow stream was flowing out of the tunnel. We entered the

Melting glacier.

interior. The most amazing thing was the light. It had an intense sky-blue colour. We were immersed in it. The ice walls were gleaming with unearthly light. The light-blue gleam accompanied us far into the depths of the glacier. It gradually faded as the ice layer above our heads was getting thicker. We were far from the edge of the glacier. Finally, we got to the place where the narrowing corridor plunged into darkness.

'OK, we can't go any further. Enough is enough. We shouldn't go deeper without proper equipment.' The ice caves were nothing unusual for Szymon, they were his 'daily bread', but I was tempted to walk on. Eventually, common sense prevailed. After all, the heavy ceiling could collapse at any minute, burying our spacious tunnel and us with it. We turned back.

'Just look at the walls. They are a masterpiece of nature.' Szymon stopped close to the exit where there was a lot of light. You could see intricate designs in the ice walls. The picture was three dimensional. You were able to see not only the surface,

Feasts of ice crystals.

but you could actually look inside the walls. Subsequent sets showed elaborate and sophisticated structures and networks of scratches, cracks, sealed crevasses, interwoven ice crystals, trapped air bubbles or miniature ducts with flowing water. There were also numerous stones, even rock blocks frozen in the ice. The rocky giants were hung in the transparent body of the glacier, able to disregard the principle of gravity. They looked as if they were hovering in midair. In addition to that, there were dark stains of fine loamy mud, which got into the ice and were frozen there for thousands of years. The whole fascinating world of the glacial interior.

'You see, this is your "favourite" moraine,' Szymon pointed to the rocks and silt trapped in the crystal clear structures, 'It looks quite harmless here.' Szymon was mocking my previous struggle with moraine morass. I had to admit he was right. The moraine looked just beautiful here. I could not take my eyes off it. It was a masterpiece of Arctic art. I relished the absolute silence that was filling the tunnel. It was interrupted only by the patter of water drops splashing against the crystal walls and floor of the cave.

It was time for us to go back. We were far away from home and wanted to catch high tide this time.

We chose a slightly different way back. We were walking closer to Torell, along its lateral wall. Although we had not planned any stops, one place drew our attention for a long time. It was a real beauty spot. The whole place seemed to be a natural exhibition hall. It was full of ice sculptures. They were lying at the foot of Torell's wall, dozens of them, in various shapes and sizes, the biggest ones being ten or 15 metres high. There must have been a massive ice-slide from the glacier. You could see a niche in it that had a much more intense blue colour than its surroundings. While looking at the diverse forms of those ice figures it was difficult to believe they were not carved by human hand. In front of us we could see two polar bears, each in their natural size, with their noses turned up. Just next to them was a seal cheerfully waving its flipper. Further on, there was an eagle with its wings unfurled, as if captured in the photograph. The diversity of the ice world revealed itself as a crystal menagerie.

We finally arrived at the spot where we had left our boat. I had to put on that miserable survival suit again. There was one more difficult manoeuvre to perform. I just hoped in my secret heart that it was the last one during that expedition.

'We'll do it this way. You take hold of the boat while I jump in and start the engine. Then you join me quickly. The current is very strong. If we don't set off at full speed, we'll be thrown out of the river channel in no time. You understand? Will you manage to jump into the boat?'

'Of course, I will.' What other thing could I possibly say? I was standing in the water up to my thighs and I had no idea how I was going to do that yet. However, the vision of the boat crashing against the stony riverbanks and vanishing in brownish muddy rapids was so nightmarish that I knew I couldn't fail.

'Watch out! I'm starting up. Jump now!'

Everything was happening so quickly that I don't have a clear memory of what happened next. I don't know what force made me kick off the ground and roll over into the boat but I did it! In such extreme situations instinct and adrenaline work more effectively than all well thought out strategies.

'Wow! I didn't know you were such a stuntwoman. What a professional leap!' This time Szymon wasn't sneering at all. His admiration was sincere. After all, we managed to set out safely, the engine was working, I was sitting in the boat and everything was going according to plan. But we got carried away by the current nonetheless. We were going at breakneck speed in that tiny boat. I saw the opposite riverbank coming towards us in dizzying motion. At the very last moment we managed to take an avoiding turn and go on.

Fortunately, the river mouth was very near. We got out onto the open sea. What a relief! We were surrounded by peace and quiet again but still filled with powerful emotions. We were slowly recovering after our white-water 'boating trip'. The tide was high, exactly as we wanted it to be, so we had no trouble mooring our boat in the port. Then, the last few steps to walk – and after hours of our expedition – we finally saw the red roof of Werenhus. Its bright colour stood out distinctly against the tundra background. It was so good to be back home again.

Werenskiold Glacier was nowhere near Torell's greatness and magnitude, not only because of its size or location. It was situated just behind our hut. It was our 'home glacier' or 'domesticated glacier', which we knew so well. First of all, it did not make such a strong impression, as it did not break off abruptly with a cliff but ended in quite an inconspicuous way. Just merging with the land. No spectacular walls, ice pillars or turrets towering over the sea. It was simply getting flatter and flatter. Its surface was cut through by more and more stream channels flowing out of it. Then it spread flat, completely turning into watery slush and creating hundreds of further brooklets. The boundary between the ice and bedrock was not definite. It was blurred and vague. It could not match the mighty barriers of Torell or Hans Glaciers. On the other hand, Werenskiold was much easier to climb. What's more, you could easily walk on its surface. Many times we wandered to its birthplace, the vast firn field, just below Kosiba pass. You could still see there the remains of the old glacial station that

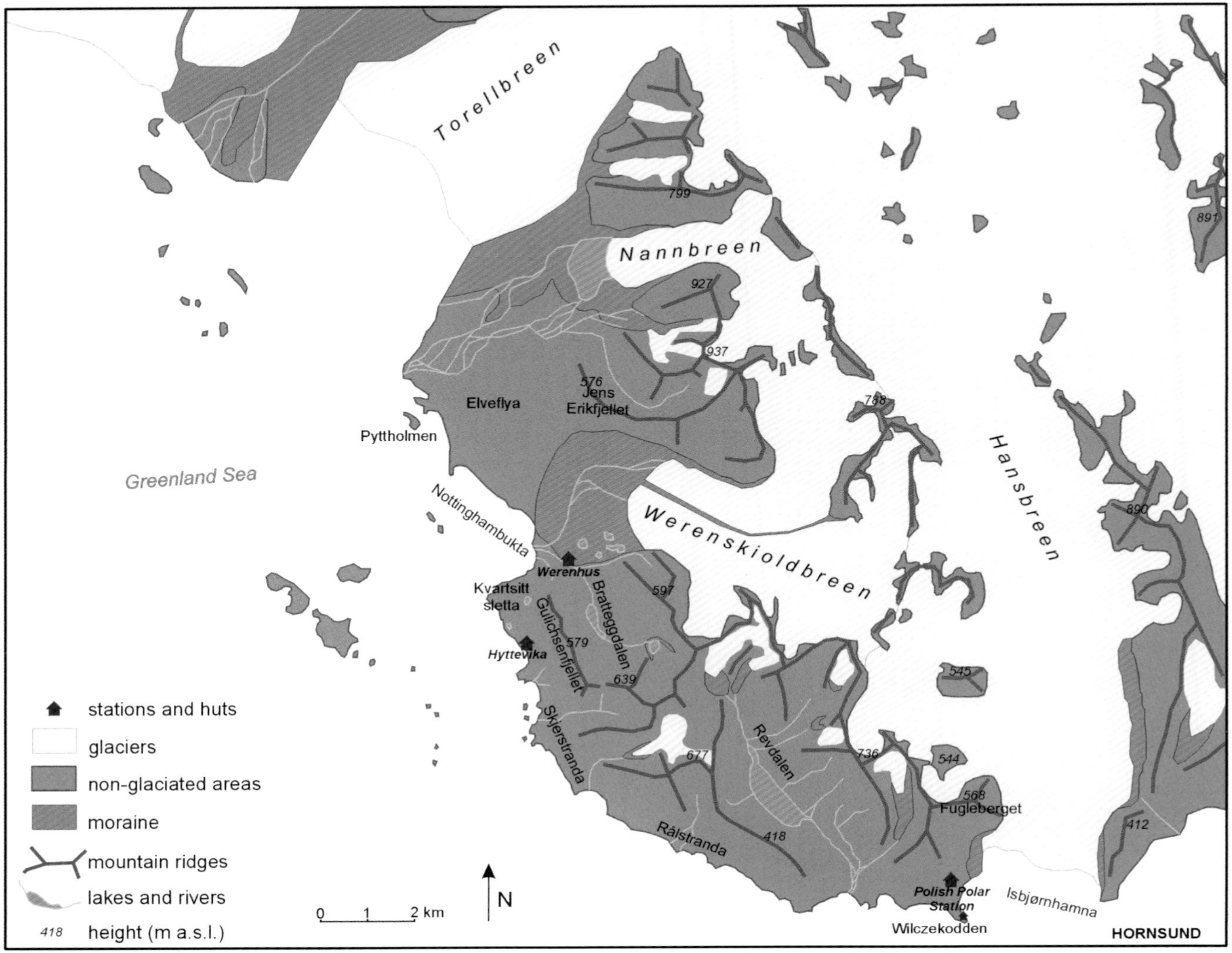

Hornsund

stations and huts
glaciers
non-glaciated areas
moraine
mountain ridges
lakes and rivers
418 height (m a.s.l.)

N

0   1   2 km

Greenland Sea

Torellbreen

Nannbreen

Pyttholmen

Elveflya

Nottinghambukta

Kvartsitt
sletta

Werennus
Jens
Eriksfjellet
576

Bratteggdalen
597

Gulichsenfjellet
579

Hyttevika

Werenskioldbreen

937
921
799

788

Hansbreen

890

891

545

568
544
Fugleberget

736

Revdalen

677

639

Skjerstranda

418

Rakstranda

Polish Polar
Station

Wilczekodden

Isbjørnhamna

HORNSUND

Above: Our ship, Horizon II, *on the water of Polar Bear Bay.*

Below: Arriving at Hornsund – Hans Glacier welcomes us.

Above: Pure magic.

Below: Slopes are active – accumulation of large talus cones and traces of debris flows.

Above: Mystical fog.

Below: Dangerous meanders of the icy cold streams on the Werenskiold Glacier.

Floating ice shines in the midnight sun.

Our neighbour in Hyttevika for the day.

Polish Polar Station in Hornsund.

Above: The Lake of Crystals in the Brattegg valley.

Below: Polar Bear Bay with Hans Glacier in the background.

Above: The double Arctic – the mirrored worlds.

Below: The bay of Hyttevika and the old trapper house.

Above: The foreland of Werenskiold Glacier consists of grey mud, stones and ice.

Below: Pack ice is terrifying and fascinating at the same time.

Above: The river of ice – Hans Glacier from a bird's eye view (from the top of the Fugle mountain).

Below: Revdalen (Rev valley).

The mighty front of Hans Glacier with collapsing (calving) ice blocks.

The Arctic can be very green and soft.

Hyttevika – the old trapper house; for me it is one of the most magical places in the world.

The Norwegian ice-breaker helped us to get through the barrier of the pack ice.

Above left: Who would dare to walk through the cracks and crevasses at the Hans Glacier front?

Above right and below: Dangerous manoeuvres among the floating ice.

Right: Walking on the edge – next step ends in the deep gorge of an icy-cold stream (Werenskiold Glacier).

Below: A complicated and dynamic geological story can be read from the rocks.

The mighty front of the Torell Glacier.

Collapsed entrance to one of the ice caves in Torell Glacier.

Polar foxes were funny companions during our walks across the tundra.

Above left: We cooked soup using the mushrooms collected in the tundra.

Above right: Collapsing glacier.

Below: The mighty Torell Glacier .

Polar poppy.

had been built directly onto the surface of the glacier. It was a sort of predecessor to our Werenhus.

The further you went up Werenskiold, the more interesting its surface was. It became more and more diverse. You could not look down on it any more, you started to respect it. Every now and then, we came across extremely deep but narrow stream channels. They cut the ice surface into an irregular 'chessboard'. In the channel walls we could see different layers. They were like dermatoglyphics or fingerprint lines of the glacier – revealing its unique history. The blue and white meant ice. The dark colour was rock dust that rolled down the slopes or was swept over the glacier's surface by the wind and then covered by subsequent layers of snow. You could hear the rapids reverberate at the bottom of those deep ravines. Those yawning precipices of the stream channels were meandering like regular rivers on the land. In some places the streams cascaded down from high above or formed impressive waterfalls. They would fall down from ice steps, ten or fifteen metres high, and create deep wells and potholes. When I came to their edges I felt dizzy. I am not sure exactly if it was due to the height of the precipice or the noise made by the rapids, or simply because my imagination was working, and I could envision what might happen if I put one careless step forward.

The water made an equally strong impression, which we could hear but not see. It was flowing somewhere beneath our feet in the ice tunnels and corridors of some indeterminate size. How thick was the ice layer between our boots and huge empty spaces below? Was it strong enough to carry us safely over the invisible streams? We were lucky each time. We tried to be extra careful. We were able to see only the exterior of the glacier, but we were aware of its elaborate interior, full of forms and shapes we could only imagine. Although we could not see it, it was enough to evoke our respect for it.

Quite a different picture of the glaciers could be gained from the mountain tops. If you climbed Fugleberget (568 metres above the sea level), the peak located in the closest vicinity of the base or Ariekammen ridge (512 metres above the sea level), a very unusual landscape would lay before your eyes. On the one side there were the dark-blue depths of the sea and shore sparkling with green and brown colours. On the other side, towards the land, there was a barrier of mountains. It was just behind this that a completely different world began. A limitless space of ice and rocks. The universe composed solely of black and white contrasts. The ice tongues coming down from the mountain valleys merged in the central part into one massive

Bird's eye view on the Hans Glacier (view from the top of the Fugle mountain).

body of white glacier. Only in some places were there single peaks of the highest mountains standing out above the ice surface. They looked like solitary islands. Their dark rocky slopes were showing up against the sparkling white background. The rest of the former world was sealed with a thick ice layer. There was just ice and rocks, white and black, up to the horizon.

The biggest glacier situated near the station, Hans Glacier, seemed to be very smooth and level on the surface in its upper part. However, when you looked at its lower part, below Fugle peak, it looked rough and uneven. Especially its end section that met the sea. As if fearing its fate, the glacier rippled and creased. It was cracking into hundreds of deep crevasses, which formed regular and symmetrical semi-circles. Those gently curved formations indicated a different pace of movement in the central and lateral parts of the glacier. They were separated from one another by craggy ridges of bent and stacked ice masses. A deadly maze for any adventurer who would venture inside during the summer. It was an ice obstacle course. Only in the winter, when snow filled up all the crevasses and built 'bridges' over them, could you penetrate the front of the glacier. But looking at it from the safe distance of Fugle peak, you could just admire the harmony between chaos and regularity in the ice forms and structures.

The ice around us also took tiny, even dainty shapes. On the surface of some lakes, located high in the mountains, frost created densely packed and drifting ice match-sticks. At the stronger gusts of wind the crystal 'bells' would strike one another and chime. You could hear some delicate heavenly music over the lake. When viewing the sea, on the other side, there were ice blocks and ice shards floating on its surface. They were shimmering with white, light-blue and greenish colours or they were completely transparent. Sometimes the waves would throw the piles of trinkets, with their sophisticated designs, onto the shore. Those tiny ornaments made the biggest noise. You could hear them crack all the time. Whether on land or in the sea they were constantly popping – releasing the trapped air bubbles that had once been enclosed within the ice crystals and kept under enormous pressure. It is this cracking ice from the glaciers that is served with whisky in some luxurious restaurants. When we were celebrating our friend's 50th birthday, a group of brave men was delegated to bring that popping ice straight from Werenskiold glacier. We wanted to drink a toast to Staszek ('Stashek') – the birthday boy – and honour him by this exceptional ice containing air bubbles, thousands of years old. The atmosphere was cracking, too.

While we were working in the field, especially on warm sunny days, we could hear again and again heavy thuds resounding. They sounded like cannon shots or the rumble of thunderbolts in a summer storm. The sound of ice blocks collapsing into the sea was carried far away on the water surface, magnified by the echo bouncing against rocky slopes of the mountain ranges. The glaciers were calving. The tonnes of ice mass were caving in, falling into the sea and making spectacular fountains of water. It was a rare sight to behold. Mostly you could just hear them. The glaciers let us know they were still alive and on the move. They did not want us to be misled by their apparent paralysis or to think they were dormant.

11 Wind

Now, after the expedition, it turns out that I cannot see that scenery any longer.
The only thing I have in my mind is a deep experience (...).

Per Olof Sundman, *The Arctic Ocean*

The wind is a constant companion in Arctic wandering. Along with the mist and drizzle, it makes up the almighty trinity in the pantheon of Spitsbergen weather deities. Windless days are very rare, they happen once in a blue moon and that's why they are so cherished. As for the daily routine, you get accustomed to the extremely changeable and unpredictable nature of your 'fair-wind' friend. At times gentle, so that you can barely feel his kiss on your cheek, on other occasions he spits raindrops with fury right into your face. Then, all of a sudden, he deals you a savage blow, taking your breath away. After several weeks spent in Spitsbergen during our second expedition we had familiarised ourselves with that windy restless spirit well enough not to react to his sudden mugging. We learned how to put up with his unruly pranks impeding work in the open air. We were able to walk long distances collecting research material even when the treacherous wind was blowing our hats away. Well, such is his nature, we could do nothing but get used to it. The way you get used to people with whom you share your dwelling – you distance yourself from initial irritable details, you simply stop noticing them. The bond is being forged and what follows is full acceptance. We thought our friendship with the Arctic wind had reached that stage. And just when it seemed to us that we had tamed the unbridled rascal and we could ignore him, he took us by surprise, unleashing a power we had not known before.

There was no harbinger of the oncoming apocalypse. It seemed it was a typical series of days of perfectly normal Spitsbergen weather that we had experienced many times before. Thick wisps of mist blurred the boundaries between tundra, rocky slopes and sky. All came together into one picture, out of focus, in all shades of grey, with a smudged outline. Impressionism in its gloomiest version. In addition to that, the unremitting drizzle. You scarcely see it through the window, but out you go and it silently creeps upon you with freezing cold. It is not an intense downpour that passes as quickly as it came. Oh no, drizzle is much worse because it is persistent and relentless. It is not its force but tenacity that can exhaust even the most 'weatherproof' man. And then comes the wind, the third element of the Spitsbergen weather. In the first days of that sequence of grey gloomy days, the wind was not that strong but we were beginning to feel its power. Day by day, it was getting worse. Thank goodness, we were nearing the end of our stay and all our field work was almost finished. There were some details to be completed but still having a couple of days in reserve we were hopefully waiting for the weather to improve. After a month of daily struggle with the conditions outside, we could not gather strength to face a few more hours in the wind, drizzle and bitterly cold mist. Tiredness made our life a misery and the threshold of our endurance decreased considerably. And it was not just resistance to the unfavourable weather conditions that failed but rather our willingness and motivation to work further. Nobody would admit to that openly, but all field teams somehow unanimously decided to adopt a wait-and-see policy. After all, we still had a couple of days left. There was no need for panic. At least there was some time to stay in and sort out our notes. At that time we did not expect, however, that until the very day of our departure we would be forced to deal only with our field 'homework' and household chores.

And so the last week at Werenhus began. Every day the weather was getting less and less favourable, not only to carry out field work but just to poke your head out of the door. Going out of the shelter was out of the question. During the next few days the wind was blowing relentlessly 24 hours a day. From behind the safe barrier of recently installed, brand-new, tightly closed windows we were staring at raging nature. The banners were flapping, being torn and ripped by the relentless wind. We watched their edges fray, single threads fly away, give into the force of the wind until one day a flag was blown away and other things followed. The next item taken was a propeller belonging to one of the two mini wind-power plants located on the moraine hill behind the hut. It is the wind that moves the windmill sails, so no wonder the propeller gave in to its power so easily. Then, the wind dance attracted litter that had been carefully collected in a metal barrel awaiting removal. The wind, however, sneered at our meticulous litter collection procedure. In just one second the barrel was not only blown a couple of metres away but also its content started to whirl around in the air over our domesticated part of the tundra. Watching the raging power of the gale we still felt safe inside our little hut. We believed that its wooden walls were able to protect us against the destructive inclinations of the wind. Our faith was tested on the day when the walls of Werenhus began to shake, and several plates and mugs fell from the kitchen shelves. They smashed to smithereens. The walls were creaking and vibrating at every strong gust of wind. With heavy hearts we listened to the house heaving sighs, hoping to goodness that the wooden boards of the thin walls and roof would endure one more gust. And another, and the next one. We knew that fun and games were over. From now on everything was in earnest. There was no talk of going outside. Forget it. Some details of our work had to remain incomplete. Our plans, ambitions, noble intentions had to yield to the power of nature. The nature that in the Arctic world shows us, continuously, that not always can we be the masters of our own fate. Not everything can be thoroughly planned and predicted. Very often you have to give up and you must resign yourself to the impossibility of fulfilling your plans. You may rebel, complain, curse the unfavourable weather but that does not change much. And there is no defeat or failure in that. It's just life – with full acceptance of human weakness and powerlessness against the power of nature.

We came to terms with our failed plans and unrealised ambitions. What began to worry us more and more was our journey back home. The date of our ship's departure from Hornsund was inevitably approaching while we were stuck here, 16 kilometres away, behind the barrier of the raging wind. We deluded ourselves into believing that the wind was going to abate by the time we had to set off from Werenhus. However, the weather forecasts that reached us from the base left no hope.

Eventually, the day came when nothing could be put off any longer. We needed to set out on our journey back home, with all our luggage on our backs, straight into the clutches of the wind. We walked in a group. Our Wroclaw ('Vrotslove') University team was joined by Cracow AGH University people from Hyttevika. The awareness of other people around you, who were struggling with the elements the way you were, gave you the strength and willpower to go on, which would have been much more difficult if you had walked alone. When you fell over, driven by a strong blast of the wind and burdened with a heavy backpack, and could not stand up, somebody else from the group would reach out their hand and help you get up, battling the wind that was trying to press you against the ground. I shall never forget the strong grip that left bruises on my hand, without which, however, I would not have been able to rise from my knees. We could not speak as the wind thrust our words back into our mouths. But we needed no words. The extended hand and strong grip were the most important thing.

The way dragged on – seemingly for an eternity. We had travelled across it so many times before, walking casually, getting used to it, talking or admiring the landscape. Now, it was different. Every step was a struggle; every metre forward was paid with sweat and some tears. All the effort of our bodies was focused on one thing – how to put the next step forward without being pushed over or backwards. It was no easy task. The wind was beating us with such rage that when I was trying to lift my foot to go on I was immediately losing my balance and had to take some steps backwards to prevent myself from falling. We staggered like drunkards in the rhythm of the wind playing around with us. To make matters worse, the ground was very uneven with stones, peat tufts and marshes of the tundra. And on top of that we had around 20 kilogrammes on our backs and the wind was whipping us with drizzle. If that physical abuse was meant to be another lesson in humility, then we humbly learnt that lesson.

The journey overland finally ended, despite my doubts if it ever would. Exhausted, dead tired, soaked with rain and sweat, achy all over and dirty as pigs from falling onto the stony and marshy ground, red-faced – we entered the hallway of the Polar Station in Hornsund. The door closed behind us. The persistent whistling of the wind that had accompanied us for several hours ceased. What a silence! The blissful warmth of the house embraced us. No other place on earth could seem more cosy and safer to me at that time.

'Come in, come inside! Leave your backpacks in the hallway; they won't be in the way. You will be served your tea in a jiffy.' The hosts of the station took care of us immediately. I felt like a stranded sailor who after the ordeal of his long voyage finally landed on a most hospitable island. What a relief.

But our joy at being saved from the windy oceans of exhaustion and our bliss at a safe haven did not last long.

'Boarding the ship is not possible for the time being. The departure from Hornsund will certainly be delayed. We don't know exactly when we can transport you to the ship.'

Rejoicing over reaching our safe haven, we had completely forgotten that it was just the first stage of the journey. There was still a ship to board and many hours of sea voyage, and the plane due to take off from Longyearbyen in less than 24 hours. But the wind would not abate. Tension was back. The lesson of humility was to be continued. Now it was the waiting. Waiting for the wind to drop, for smaller waves in the sea, for the captain's decision to board the ship, for sailing out of the bay. Again, nothing depended on us. We could fret, worry, panic, glance at our watches nervously and count the dangerously shrinking hours to the departure of our plane. All that did not make any difference. Well, maybe it affected our mood, which became more and more sombre. The stress of helpless expectation infected everybody. And everything was supposed to be so beautiful. The whole day room at the base had been prepared for the reception of the guests arriving on the ship – the captain and his crew were to come. The station was to celebrate the arrival of the ship and reunion of people. The cook with his helpers did a great job, and the tables put along the wall tempted us with an aromatic and colourful variety of dishes. They were also waiting for the party to begin. But it never did. The lettuce wilted, sliced meats and cheeses went dry, sophisticated appetisers served on cocktail sticks somehow contracted, and the desire to have a good time waned. The base was instead filled with a heavy atmosphere of tense waiting. Conversations dropped, people scattered, sat down in armchairs, winter explorers disappeared in their rooms. We lapsed into lethargy, broken from time to time by radio communication with the ship. The messages were still adverse. The hour of boarding was being delayed. The wind was still too strong and the waves far too big to sail into the bay with people and luggage. The only thing we could do was to wait longer.

Suddenly an order came! The wind had temporarily abated and the loading could be carried out. Quick! No time to waste. Nobody knows how long the peaceful conditions are going to last. In one second the inertia turned into haste and confusion. Panicky actions, excitement, running about, commotion, shouts. After a while quite a big group of summer explorers and winter explorers seeing us off headed for the shore, where our PTS boat was being started. In no time we and our luggage boarded. The boat dipped its tracks in the water and soon it was rolling on the waves. The wind had really dropped. We were getting closer and closer to the ship anchored in the middle of Polar Bear Bay. Our salvation seemed so near! The atmosphere was good on the PTS boat. We were joking and having fun in our naive belief that we were over the worst now. The blue stripe on the port side of *Horizon II* was within reach.

Then came an unexpected blow. The wind attacked with redoubled strength. All around us suddenly grew giant waves, appearing out of the blue or rather out of the rippled surface of the water. The large yellow body of the amphibious vehicle, normally used in much more peaceful conditions, with no ambition to be a wave breaker, started to shudder nervously. The bigger and bigger waves were swelling in front of the boat, plunging with great force onto the open deck, soaking us and our luggage. The metal giant was giving in to the waves as if it was a plastic toy in a child's bathtub. We shared its fate going up and down, feeling on our skin, through soaked clothes, the ice-cold touch of water streams sweeping the deck. The ship, however, was much closer than the coastline, so we kept sailing. Finally, one of the waves tossed the PTS boat against the ship's side. It made a dent, a dark scratch, a weal. Soon there was a rope ladder dropped from the ship and our evacuation began in haste. We were all rushing but in such rough seas and with uncontrolled swaying of both the ship and amphibian – climbing up the ladder was no easy job. But we managed. We all climbed onto the deck of *Horizon II* and then began loading our luggage. Just then the hawser broke. The PTS boat, propelled by a previously stretched rope, was abruptly carried away by one of the giant waves. There was no coming back. The waves were much too big to risk approaching the broadside. PTS had to go back to the coast as soon as possible to avoid sinking. We watched the yellow spot recede further and further on the rough surface of the dark sea, taking our luggage away.

Again, we could do nothing about it. Our fury, cursing, outbreaks of anger, tears were of no consequence as they could not change anything. Once again we had to submit to the elements and wait. We could only hope that the rough sea would calm down and our luggage would be transferred onto the ship. Time was flying and the hour of our flight departure was inexorably getting closer. The only obstacle was that there were still many hours of sea voyage between us and our target. Not to mention the storm. The captain decided that we should wait a little bit longer in the bay. However, if the weather did not change, we would have to go without our luggage. It was good that at least we had our hand luggage, small rucksacks containing the most important belongings primarily our documents, ID cards and plane tickets.

Our ship, Horizon II, *on the water of Polar Bear Bay.*

'Our tickets are inside one of the backpacks that returned to the base!' sounded a despairing voice of a member of Cracow AGH University team, who had just taken in the fullness of their calamity.

'So what now?! What now?!' Panic spread like wildfire.

'You shouldn't have left your most important documents in the big luggage! You are supposed to be grown-ups and serious scientists and you've acted so foolishly!' The crew were more critical than sympathetic.

After a while something worse was realised. One of the explorers had left in his big luggage essential medicines that he had to take regularly. The situation was getting more and more complicated. In the meantime the wind was unleashing its fury at the sea and in the skies, mocking our human dramas and dilemmas. We were all sitting in the mess in the lower part of the ship as there were no cabins provided for us. We were just supposed to travel a short distance to Longyearbyen. I suppose in a normal situation I wouldn't mind that at all. But at that particular moment, after such strong emotions and enormous stress, the lack of my own little nook in which I could lay my weary head was most acute. Luckily, later on we found some free single bunks in cabins.

When the tension subsided, I felt cold. I was drenched to my skin and I wasn't the only one. Our clothes were soaking wet and spare ones, dry ones, were far away. My friend Sikor (nicknamed Titmouse), who was one of the few fortunate travellers who had taken their big backpacks from the PTS boat, made the grade now. He distributed his dry garments among dripping wet and frozen people gathered in the mess. All came in handy – socks, long johns, T-shirts, fleece jackets and so on. This spontaneous impulse to share everything he had in his rucksack let in some sunshine and cheered us up a bit. Once more on that day a helping hand meant more than any words – especially as Titmouse kept grumbling and mumbling how foolish we were not to take our luggage straight away from the boat. Reproaching us for that, he continued to provide everyone with further dry items of clothing. Spiteful remarks sounded softer when accompanied with a pair of warm woollen socks.

'Take them, change them quickly!' His rough commanding voice could not lessen my gratitude to him.

'Thanks a million, Titmouse. You are great!'

'Oh, shut up! Just take off your wet socks or you'll catch a cold. I just don't get how you lot didn't manage to take your backpacks off the boat but wasted your precious time on goodbying!' Yes, Titmouse wouldn't be himself if he didn't take advantage of the situation and didn't make some critical comments. However, pulling on his much oversized socks, I felt I could forgive him any irony.

Once again we had to wait. Questions arose: 'Will they be able to transport our luggage?' 'Will we be able to set off in this stormy weather at all?' 'Will we arrive in time for the plane?' They remained unanswered. The only thing we were able to do was to wait and hope.

'Dinghies are coming! Two dinghies.' Our apathy was suddenly disturbed by an uplifting shout given out by some intent observers. 'The winter explorers are bringing our stuff!'

So it turned out well. All the luggage was brought safely onto the deck. The owners were overjoyed. Especially the Cracow people, who were over the moon about their recovered tickets and prospects of flying back home.

I was standing on the deck. The ship was being tossed on the waves, which did not get much smaller. I was looking at the dinghies sailing off towards the shore. They had completed their rescue mission. Their red colour contrasted with the dark sheet of rough sea. I don't even know which of the winter explorers came to us then, but I was deeply moved. I was grateful for their bravery and sacrifice. For their unhesitating response and conviction that it was the *right thing* to do. And so they did it, without asking unnecessary questions or 'making a profit and loss account' first. It was just another example within just 24 hours of how extreme situations and real danger release in people much goodness, courage and sacrifice. Paradoxically, in the most dramatic situations, when it seems that we should first of all save our own skin, we are capable of the most altruistic deeds. We show courage to act selflessly and sacrifice ourselves for others.

Suddenly the ship jerked abruptly. At the last possible moment I took hold of the sideboard. Our backpacks scattered.

'What's up?!' We looked at one another with growing fear.

We soon realised what was going on. The ship was no longer just going up and down, yielding to the oncoming crests and troughs of the waves. We were drifting. With a sudden gust of wind the ship was no longer lying at anchor, it was being carried towards the rocky shores. I don't think we fully understood the gravity of the situation. But those who did had already given commands and started to act. The engines wailed and strained, the drifting was stopped and the heavy hull of the ship began making its way against the wind in the opposite direction. We could hear the clatter of the anchor being pulled up. We were sailing off, leaving Polar Bear Bay in a full storm. The ship tried to rear up several times, it heeled dangerously from side to side. Keeping balance while standing was almost impossible. All loose items left in the cabins were rolling from one side to the other, bouncing against the walls.

Before I came down with seasickness and was bedridden, or rather 'bunkridden', until the end of our voyage, I spent some time on the captain's bridge. There was quite a big group of people gathered there. No wonder, it was the best place from which to safely admire the elements around us. In front of us the ship bow broke wave after wave, going up and then down as if in an amusement park. But there was nothing amusing about this.

'Have a look!' The first officer beckoned us over to the navigating board. 'This is the record of the wind force,' he pointed to a ragged chart. 'Can you see? We have run out of scale… The wind was gusting up to 70 kilometres per hour. We were in the centre of a hurricane. Just when you set off in the PTS boat – you found yourselves in the eye of the hurricane. After a short spell of calmness, the wind started to blow from the opposite direction. It was exactly then, when the waves started to roll over the deck. You shouldn't have been at sea then at all. But nobody could have predicted that. You know, one bigger wave could have done away with you. PTS boats are not fit for sailing in such weather conditions. One strong sweep and they go under. You've been damn lucky!'

I was listening in amazement. I could see the same disbelief mixed with fear in my friends' eyes. We were completely unaware of the fact that we had just had a brush with something more powerful than a sea storm. While the waves were sweeping over our PTS boat, we just worried about our clothes getting soaked or our dripping wet backpacks. That was all we were concerned about. Such trivial things – from the present perspective – occupied our minds then. Maybe it was good. It is sometimes better not to know the truth, not to be aware of it. I can hardly say how I would have felt if I had known then it was not just wet clothes I should worry about, but whether I would again see the people dear to me. A completely different perspective. Later, I reflected on something else. It is so easy to stop living. One big wave is enough and that's the end. Everything goes under the water – all your joy and success, worries and failures, big and small fears, minor and major issues, happy and sad memories, your hopes, dreams and disappointments. Nothing exists any longer. Due to one big wave. You never know when it may come or what form it may take. We did not know at that time either that it was so real and close to us. That is the reason why you should never put off any ambition, dream or happiness for later. Nor should you ever hesitate to reach out a helping hand to another person.

The wind and rough sea accompanied us to the very end of our voyage. The majority of us spent it lying on our bunks as motionless as possible or locked up in the toilets. But we did manage to catch our plane. It did take off in spite of the considerable strength of the wind. Just think. Everything started from an innocent breeze a week ago. Nobody could have predicted that our constant companion in Arctic wandering would turn into a fierce enemy bringing near destruction. But this is the Arctic – unpredictable and astonishing the moment you think you have tamed it. You cannot be more mistaken if you think you have. More often than not you realise that you are in the hands of nature, and depend on her generosity. A constant lesson of humility has to be patiently learned.

A 'homemade' wind power station at Werenhus.

12 The sacred

Now I know that remembering what you have seen is not possible,
The only thing you retain in your memory is the feeling of your incapability to remember.

Per Olof Sundman, *The Arctic Ocean*

How relative is experiencing anything.

Jan Jozef Szczepanski, *The Polar Bear Bay*

'At eleven o'clock we set off for Wilczek ('Veeltchek').'[3] It is a buzzword or signal spread all over the base. Its meaning is being explained to polar novices. Before the arranged hour the majority of permanent and temporary residents of the base set out for nearby Cape Wilczek. Some people, especially regulars of Hornsund, take candles with them.

'We set off for Wilczek' is not a call for a hunting expedition or some illegal or secret gathering. It is a sign that Sunday has come.

At the very end of Wilczek headland, in which direction the whole group strolls, there is a wooden cross. Its slim, tall shape stands out distinctly against the sky and sea. When you are on the boat coming to Polar Bear Bay, the first sight that you see is the cross on Cape Wilczek. It appears before you can actually see the buildings of the Polar Station of Polish Academy of Sciences. It is an unmistakable sign that you are nearing the end of your journey.

---

3   Wilczek is a surname of an Austrian Arctic explorer: Johann Nepomuk Graf Wilczek. The word 'wilczek' also means 'a young wolf'. So the expression used in Polish implies setting off for a hunting expedition for a wolf.

A small shrine and altar at Cape Wilczek in Hornsund.

The cross was erected on one of the rocks on the headland. To make it more stable, a cairn was built at its foot. In the lower part of the cross someone hung a small shrine. Inside, protected from the sea and wind, there is a holy figure made by a folk artist, who with a few decisive cuts carved the saddened face of Jesus out of driftwood. The wood went grey, dry and eventually cracked. A wide scar cuts the face, deepening its sadness. Next to the cross there is a small altar table. It is also grey and wooden. Rarely is the mass said here, mostly at Easter or Christmas, when the weather makes it possible for the Norwegian pastor to visit the winter explorers' team. But in the history of this unusual temple there were also remarkable events when, for example, the primate of Poland, cardinal Jozef Glemp, came to hold mass, or a ceremony of marriage was held here.

Most often the Sunday service is held in complete silence and concentration, with a small group of people standing around the cross. Each of us would hold an individual conversation, in our thoughts, with the Almighty. The candles placed on the rocks and stones around the altar flicker in the wind. They burn for our special intentions, spoken only in our secret hearts.

In this extraordinary 'chapel' on Cape Wilczek it does not matter what kind of religion you profess, what country you originate from or what language you speak. It is not important. The Norwegian Protestant pastor celebrating the service for Catholic Poles is not the only example. Even people who are far from church-going tradition set off for Wilczek headland and remain there for some time in contemplation. It is a special place to everyone – the sacred place. Some people perceive 'the sacred' in the symbol of the cross pointing towards the sky, while others find it in the mightiness of the surrounding Arctic nature. The temple at Wilczek has no walls, no definite boundaries or limits. It is open to the surrounding space, it becomes united with it. Maybe because of that, in this special place you can feel this exceptional unity of our human needs, desires and intentions, which turn out to be the same if you reject all external limitations, artificial divisions and facades.

This supra-religious dimension of the sacred space at Cape Wilczek can also be seen in various plaques made of stone, metal or wood. These plaques are epitaphs of those who died in the Arctic, but are also to give thanks for survival, for being able to live on. In this respect, we come close to the most important issues for us, the topics of life and death. After all, that is what matters in the final 'settlement'. Both of them release in us the need to be near the sacred, whatever it means to each of us.

The cross on Cape Wilczek also has another meaning. It was erected by Polish winter explorers during the expedition in 1981–1982. The convergence of dates with political changes and the Solidarity movement in Poland's recent history is no coincidence. The construction of the cross was to symbolise the protest against the martial law introduced in Poland in 1981. The universal 'sacred' was closely tied with the individual history of the nation and very earthly matters.

Our Sunday contemplation at the cross at Wilczek comes to an end. One by one, people walk back towards the station. The mystery of common and joint experience of the sacred is fulfilled. But you do not go straight back to the base. On the way you make one more stop in a wooden hut, the so-called 'policeman's house'. Now it is time to celebrate, time to talk with others, joke, laugh, exchange your viewpoint on endless subjects, before you return to your own room and your own business. I immediately think of the Polish countryside, where in traditional villages the church building was always accompanied by an inn. There must be a balance in everything. There is a time of silence and telling jokes, of experiencing the sacred, but also enjoying the world with all your senses.

13 Farewell

We were more and more deeply overcome by a feeling of ambiguity of the world,
the feeling accompanying all farewells.
Not only time seems to be undefined in such moments,
but also our attitude towards certain places
turns out to be fluid, ambiguous and full of contradictions.

Jan Jozef Szczepanski, *The Polar Bear Bay*

From the diary of my third stay in Spitsbergen:

The last day in Werenhus. In an hour and half we should leave the hut to arrive
at Hyttevika sharp at five p.m. We have made an appointment with Krzysiek
('Ksheeshek') and he is coming by boat to pick up our luggage. The atmosphere is
tense and everybody is nervous. Quick packing, chaos in the kitchen – some people
have forgotten they are on cooking duty, endless discussions about the return –
who goes with who and when, who is going by boat, who is walking to the base,
etc. – options are multiplying and changing every minute. Oh dear! These lads are
so indecisive and disorganised. I have already made up my mind. I am going to
the base on foot. I don't want to go by boat. I wish to walk one more time along
the shoreline. Maybe the last time? Who knows? Sailing to the base would be too
quick – I want to leave the world of Werenhus slowly, enjoy it in silence, breathe
the Arctic air as long as possible. I know that the moment we reach the base a

chapter of my story here will be finished. The base means a different world. I'm not longing for it, so I want to prolong the time and space suspended 'in between' (…)

I'm sitting at my favourite desk, in a small room, a so-called laboratory room. In front of me the window overlooks Brattegg river – today all in grey. The whole bay is veiled in mist. I've been to the moraine hill earlier this morning. You can't see the upper part of Bratteggdalen (Brattegg Valley) at all. Everything is enveloped in low clouds. It looks as if the world finishes on the nearest rock step. Why am I so sad to leave this foggy, damp and grey place? I thought I wasn't going to feel the farewell with Werenhus so acutely this year. After all, it has been my third summer in Spitsbergen. But I don't think you can avoid it (…)

I woke up quite early this morning, in my 'regular' sleeping place, in the furthest corner of the attic. I stared at the wooden walls and sloping ceiling low above my head. As if the most important thing was to remember each knot on the wooden planks, irregular cracks or gaps between them, the whistling wind coming through them, drops of hardened resin, all hues and shades of the wooden structure, the pattern of tree rings – once concentric, once circular like the eyes on the peacock's tail. I was doing my best to draw them beneath my eyelids, to remember everything in detail – just in case I was never to return. I listened attentively to the rustle of Brattegg waterfall. In my first days here I used to mistake it for the rain. Later, I learned to distinguish between the differing sounds. Some people were disturbed by the sound of the waterfall, they couldn't fall asleep. For me, it was just one more element of our attic bedroom, inseparably connected with that place. Just like I associate the ubiquitous sounds of little auks with my stay at Hyttevika. They accompanied us day and night being a part of the surrounding world. I'd like to encompass all these things and preserve them in my memory, to remember them forever (…)

I don't know if I will return here or come back many times to spend summer after summer within the walls of Werenhus and the vicinity of the Werenskiold Glacier. But it's possible that it is the last time I have slept in Werenhus attic and sat in front of our house. Protected from the wind on the cosy veranda I look up towards the misty valley of Bratteggdalen. I have no idea what will happen in the future, what's ahead of me. But I know it is the height of my Spitsbergen history. Even if I was never to come back here and always long for the rustle of the waterfall by Werenhus, the scent of the sea and the sound of little auks at Hyttevika, the taste *of tea and sesame biscuits (our staple diet in the field exploration), the view from the window overlooking the grey waters of Nottinghambukta (Nottingham Bay) or the wistful whistling of the wind in the slits of the hus, I know I have lived it to the full. Whatever comes next, later, in the future – I am happy that I can keep 'my own Spitsbergen'.*

It is amazing how our memory works. It recalls details. Seemingly unimportant trifles and trivialities become embedded in it. They evoke pictures full of colours, sounds, tastes and scents that are capable of recreating a different space and time – an apparently bygone era.

The ship has raised the anchor. We are slowly leaving Polar Bear Bay. It is the third time I have bid farewell to the familiar coastline. The coast is moving backwards. It is like rewinding a film. The 'film' I just saw on my way from Werenhus to the base a few hours earlier. A time from several years ago comes to my mind, when I came into Hornsund port for the first time in my life. The shoreline was new and strange to me. Rocks, valleys, peaks and streams that came into view were just neutral fragments of the landscape. I wondered then if I would ever look at them with emotions like those who had been there before and were coming back once more. Now I know the answer. There is no unfamiliar place on the coast for me any longer. I know every nook and cranny here. We pass Revdalen (Rev valley) with a wide river mouth, then the flat green shores of Rålstranda and Skjerstranda, and in the range of jagged ridges opens a wide pass – Gangpasset, just next to it the valley of Steinvikdalen (Steinvik valley), and finally Gullichsenfjellet and the bay of Hyttevika. You have to look hard to see a low-lying hut. The coastline turns, in front of us Kvartsittsletta reveals itself – the Quartzite Coast and further on is the massive body of Torell Glacier. Somewhere there, between them, is Werenhus. It is impossible to see it from the ship. But I can see it nonetheless. Its dark-green walls and the faded red of its roof. A tiny spot in the limitless space of moss, rocks and ice. Coming here for the first time I wished to tame this world, to domesticate it, to be able to think about it as 'my world'. It has happened. This space acquired a new dimension. It has become something more than just one of the Arctic shores. It has become a world in itself. For each of us a slightly different world, although on the outside it is seemingly the same. We filled up the space of the coast with our individual time and histories. The peaks, valleys, passes and glaciers mean different things to each of us. This is the magic of discover-

Just about to leave the Werenhus – the expedition comes to an end.
'See you next summer, Werenhus!'

ing new territories and becoming familiar with them. A part of that is giving names to nameless spots and corners: Lake of Crystals, Emerald Lake, Rock Castle. You will not find these names on a map, but 'the initiated', those let into the secret, will undoubtedly know where to find them.

A thicker and thicker fog is coming between us and the shoreline. Some mountain tops have already disappeared behind its curtain. But I am not leaving the deck. I am hypnotised by the coastline. In spite of the mist, my memory and imagination can perfectly add the missing fragments of the topographic picture. And I am not the only one. Several other people, like me, are gazing into the distance, at the shore dissolving into thin air. Nobody says a word. The mystery of farewell must take place in silence and solitude. Such is the law of memories, which are so elusive and personal that they cannot be conveyed.

The phenomenon of Spitsbergen consists in the complexity or multi-layered structure of the histories related to it. On the one hand, it becomes an individual experience for each of us. My polar adventure, my scientific mission consisted of working in hard conditions, meeting new people, with wild nature within my grasp, and appreciating a lesson of humility towards the Arctic environment. On the other hand, Spitsbergen is a great collective experience. It is an experience joining different generations and lasting for generations. It is an idea that has continued for several decades since the first Polish expedition set off for the Arctic. The next explorers continue to write their own unique stories, adding to this history. There is no 'one and true' history of Spitsbergen. Each person who steps ashore and is 'bitten by the Arctic bug' carries bits of this history into all parts of the world. Does it sound lofty and grandiose? Maybe. But I am not ashamed of it. I am fully aware of this extraordinary fact: we are becoming a part of this great polar history – even if our stories are short and petty in comparison with the ones of the first explorers of these territories. We could experience the Arctic not as tourists coming for a while, but as residents, people from these parts, rooted in the Arctic daily life. Whatever lays ahead in the future, this ice, the rocks, the sea and our polar friendships will be within us forever.

Vast open space.

14 Epilogue

Nothing as important was going on as to deserve a lofty name of an experience.
But all that made great sense. We had the feeling that we lived our lives to the full.

Jan Jozef Szczepanski, *The Polar Bear Bay*

I am standing on the rocky ridge of the mountain range in my home country – Poland, several thousands of kilometres south of the North Pole. The July heat wave makes itself felt. Around me there is a crowd of tourists wearing just shorts and T-shirts. Nevertheless, in spite of the summer heat and sunshine, the fresh breeze brings some cool memories. This place reminds me of the Arctic: the similarly jagged peaks; the steep slopes covered with a thick layer of coarse rock debris which will result in a rock fall if you try to tread on it, similar to its polar counterpart. Massive talus cones are cut through by deep gullies made by the sudden debris flows. These forms are only too well known from the Arctic. Most blocks and rocks are covered by green and yellow lichen, the same as those in the far North. In some places you find small light-violet flowers of saxifrages and the creeping willows, the net-leaved and dwarf willows, growing on rocks. You must beware of bears, too. Their fur is of a different colour but they are no less dangerous here. At least in Spitsbergen you have a gun to protect yourself, while here you are defenceless.

The Tatra Mountains. A small substitute for the vast Arctic environment. I am not the first one to compare my polar memories to the scenery of the Tatras. After all, we used to have glaciers here some thousands of years ago.

There is an extensive panorama from the ridge I am standing on. Visibility is perfect today. I can see clearly all the peaks of the High Tatras far into Slovakia up to the horizon. Deep valleys cut through the rocky ridges and mountainsides. The steep slopes and wide flat bottoms of the valleys reveal the former presence of glaciers. And what if I close my eyes and employ my imagination again? I fill up all the valleys with ice and snow to make them look like thousands of years ago. What's the result? A very familiar picture. In front of me extends an endless vast space of glacial fields and tongues. Above them are dark massifs of rocky peaks, standing out like lone islands in the sea, the 'ocean' of ice and rocks I admired many times from Ariekammen (Arie ridge) or Fugleberget (Fugle summit) above Hornsund Station. Now, thanks to my imagination, I can see the same landscape from the ridge of Orla Perc ('Orla Pertch') – the picture of the Tatras from the distant past. Sometime in the future, Spitsbergen glaciers will melt and leave empty suspended valleys behind. Just like these here.

Time to go back. There is quite a walk. But we can see our house from far away although this time, the roof is not red and the walls not green. But like the Spitsbergen huts it has a long history. It is a former shepherds' shelter. The sight of a small hut makes me joyful in the same way the sight of Werenhus did. After all, we are coming back home after a day's work in the field.

Finally, we have reached our Tatra 'hus'. We are inside and embrace its cosy and silent atmosphere, the scent of its wooden walls, the creaking old floor and stairs. The picture of Werenhus comes immediately to my mind. This place is also a research station that belongs to the Polish Academy of Sciences like the one in Hornsund. But now we are on the mountain pastures of the Tatra Mountains – called Hala Gasienicowa ('Haalla Gonshenitsova').

'At last you've come! What on earth took you so long? I've been waiting for you with dinner for ages.' Marek ('Mharek'), a meteorological expert, is an expert cook as well. And a great raconteur. Our common meals always turn into some kind of a social gathering. That also sounds familiar to me.

Tomorrow is my turn for cooking duty. The same rule of sharing our duties has already worked well in another place. And one more similarity – guests. Almost every day someone comes to visit us. For a day or two, or just for tea. Our friends and our friends' friends. One big family. Continuous meetings with new people. Each of them brings something new and individual to the atmosphere of the station, each of them shares something with the group. And in this particular way the climate of our temporary house is being created. It is changing like the global climate, it is getting warmer and warmer, but in this case it is not a bad thing at all. So almost everything is the same as in the far North: the rules of functioning in a small group, the celebration of certain moments, a slow pace of life and lots of other similar elements in our daily life. It turns out that you do not have to look far, the most important things are within your grasp, only waiting to be discovered. To be noticed and appreciated in your daily life. They are waiting for you to reach out your hand.

⚘   ⚘   ⚘

I know what will happen. I'll always want to come back here.
This longing will never cease.

Per Olof Sundman, *The Arctic Ocean*

LIST OF POLISH NAMES

Aga	/'aːga/ – short form of Agnieszka	**Jasiu**	/'ja: ʃiu/
		Jozef Glemp	/'juːzef/ /'glemp/
Agnieszka	/aː 'gɲieʃka/	**Jurek**	/'juːrek/
Alfred Jahn	/aːlfred jʌn/	**Kosiba**	/koˈʃiːba/
Andrzej	/'aːndʒei/	**Krzysiek**	/'kʃiː ʃek/, Christopher
Anka	/'aːnka/	**Marek**	/'maːrek/
Banachowka	/baːnaː 'huːfka/	**Mirek**	/'miːrek/
Baranowka	/baːraː 'nuːfka/	**Orla Perc**	/'orlaː/ /'pertʃ/
Bartek	/'Baːrtek/	**Sikor**	/'ʃiːkoːr/
Cytrynowka	/tsɪtrɪ 'nuːfka/	**Stanislaw Baranowski**	/sta: 'niswʌv/ /baːraː 'novskɪ/
Czarek	/'tʃaːrek/		
Czeslaw Nowicki	/'tʃeswaːv/ /noʹvɪtskɪ/	**Stanislaw Siedlecki**	/sta: 'niswʌv/ /ʃjedʹletskɪ/
Hala Gasienicowa	/'haːlaː/ /gonʃenɪ'tsoːva/	**Staszek**	/'sta: ʃek/
Heniu	/'henjuː/	**Szymon**	/'ʃimon/
Jan Jozef Szczepanski	/'jʌn/ /'juːzef/ / ʃtʃeʹpa: ŋskɪ/	**Wilczek**	/'viːltʃek/
		Wroclaw	/'vroːtswaːv/
Jarek	/'jaːrek/		

Another polar story you will enjoy ...

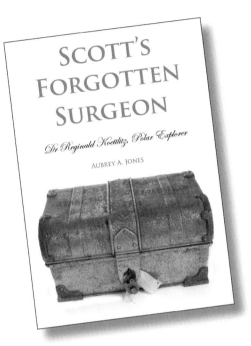

SCOTT'S FORGOTTEN SURGEON

AUBREY A. JONES

❖ An insight into the vital role played by Dr. Reginald Koettlitz during the heroic period of polar exploration

❖ Covers the four main expeditions undertaken by Koettlitz, leading up to the ill-fated Terra Nova Expedition

❖ Includes previously unseen photographs and correspondence

FROM THE REVIEWS

'...this is a remarkable book, extremely well researched and wholly enlightening. ... This thorough appraisal of a most gifted individual is well worth the price...' *The James Caird Society Newsletter*

'...this book represents a significant addition to the literature of polar exploration'. *Antarctic Book Notes*

'...captures the adventurous life and poignant love story of explorer, Dr. Reginald Koettlitz, a great man ... is a fascinating read ... rich in hitherto unpublished material ... brings the late 1800s to life...' *Rose's Round Up, South Africa*

'...the book that lifts the lid on the story of a Dover explorer lost to history'. *Kent News*

£18.99 978-184995-038-1 240 × 170mm 224 pages 70 b/w illustrations softback

Whittles Publishing, Dunbeath Mill, Dunbeath, Caithness, Scotland. KW6 6EG, UK
Tel: +44(0)1593-731 333; Fax: +44(0)1593-731 400;
e-mail: info@whittlespublishing.com • www.whittlespublishing.com

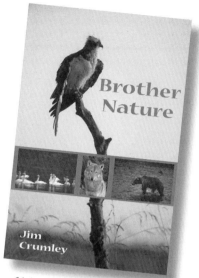
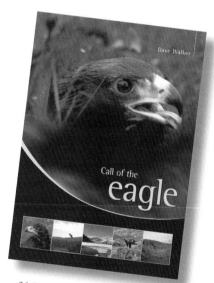
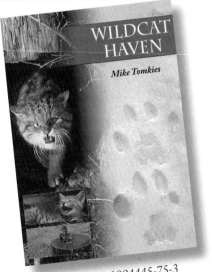